THE INNOVATION EXPEDITION

A VISUAL TOOLKIT TO START INNOVATION

Published in 2013 by
BIS Publishers
Building Het Sieraad
Postjesweg 1
1057 DT Amsterdam
T +31 (0)20 515 02 30
bis@bispublishers.nl
www.bispublishers.nl

Design
studio frederik de wal
Editing
Christine Boekholt DeLucia
ISBN 978 90 6369 313 8
Second printing 2014
Copyright 2013 © Gijs van Wulfen
and BIS Publishers, Amsterdam

THE INNOVATION EXPEDITION

A VISUAL TOOLKIT TO START INNOVATION

GIJS VAN WULFEN **BIS PUBLISHERS**

FULL STEAM AHEAD

1 INNOVATION FOCUS WORKSHOP
IDEATION TEAM
2 CORE TEAM INTRO MEETING
FORTH PLANNING
INNOVATION ASSIGNMENT
BAY OF DOUBTS: DO WE REALLY NEED TO INNOVATE?
3 KICK-OFF WORKSHOP
DEPARTURE DOCUMENT
6-10 INNOVATION OPPORTUNITIES
POTENTIAL TARGET GROUPS
FAILED BRAINSTORM WRECKS

OBSERVE & LEARN

4 EXPLORE PREPARATION WORKSHOP
BEST INNOVATION OPPORTUNITIES
6 4 OBSERVE & LEARN WORKSHOPS
5 EXPLORING TRENDS & TECHNOLOGY
AN OPEN MIND
6 DISCOVERING CUSTOMER FRICTIONS
7 EXPLORING INNOVATION OPPORTUNITIES
BEST CUSTOMER FRICTIONS

BUSY BUSY BUSY ESCAPE HARBOUR
CUSTOMERS ARE SCARY CLIFFS
BUSINESS AS USUAL SAND BANKS
WE INNOVATE ANYWAY
MY BOSS WON'T LET ME ISLAND
OUR OWN BLIND SPOTS
IT'S NOW OR NEVER CURRE
THE CALM BEFORE THE STORM PASSAGE

TEST IDEAS

12 2ND CONCEPT IMPROVEMENT WORKSHOP
4
3-5 IMPROVED TESTED CONCEPTS
11 CONCEPT TESTING

ME-TOO TRIANGLE

RAISE IDEAS

500-750 IDEAS
30-40 IDEA DIRECTIONS
9 NEW PRODUCT BRAINSTORM
3
12 IMPROVED CONCEPTS
12 CONCEPTS
10 1ST CONCEPT IMPROVEMENT WORKSHOP

POS STO
'AM I CREATIVE?' TIDE

'CUSTOMERS DON'T LIKE IT' BAY
'NOT INVENTED HERE' CLIFFS

HOMECOMING

3-5 MINI NEW BUSINESS CASES
THE BEST COACHES ARE IN THE SANDS WATCH TOWER
13 CONCEPT TRANSFER WORKSHOP
5
14 FINAL PRESENTATION
15 4 MINI NEW BUSINESS CASE WORKSHOPS
AN INNOVATIVE MINDSET
AN EFFECTIVE IDEATION PROCESS
'WE CAN DO IT' MIST

NO SUPPORT CLIFFS
WARM CREATIVE GULF STREAM

FORTH
INNOVATION METHOD

LEGEND
☼ INNOVATION CLIMATE
▸▸ STAGES
✳ ACTIVITIES
⊙ DELIVERABLES

▸▸ FULL STEAM AHEAD   5 WEE
▸▸ OBSERVE AND LEARN   6 WEE
▸▸ RAISE IDEAS   2 WEE
▸▸ TEST IDEAS   3 WEE
▸▸ HOMECOMING   4 WEE

USE THE INSPIRING
FORTH INNOVATION METHOD
TO CREATE ATTRACTIVE
INNOVATIVE PRODUCTS
AND SERVICES WITH GREAT
INTERNAL SUPPORT WITH
A MULTIDISCIPLINARY TEAM
IN YOUR ORGANIZATION

The Innovation Expedition

Innovation is highly relevant to every organization. Yet, eighty percent of innovation projects never reach the market. Many have a false start. The Innovation Expedition is written to inspire you with practical tools on HOW to start innovation effectively. This book is intended for innovators: managers, consultants, entrepreneurs and organization leaders. The process of innovation is highly relevant in their professional capacity; and it is a process that many struggle to master. *"What is the right moment?" "How do I discover what customers want?" "How do I get breakthrough ideas?" "How do I get internal support?"*

This book takes an original approach to show how you can innovate the expedition way! It draws parallels between mankind's greatest explorations in history and modern-day innovation. How Columbus discovered America; how Hillary reached the summit of Everest; and how Neil Armstrong got to be the first man on the Moon. Their remarkable stories of exploration and how they overcame unexpected setbacks will inspire you to approach innovation with a new mindset.

The Innovation Expedition is a visual toolkit for a successful start to innovation. It is 248 pages packed with accounts of historic explorations, quotes, charts, cases, checklists, formats and innovation maps. The fundamental parallels that can be drawn between historic voyages of discovery and innovation today are that: the process takes time; it's full of risks; and there will be unexpected setbacks. The book is full of practical and visual tools. And with its unusual design, The Innovation Expedition is a unique, hands-on voyage of discovery in itself.

One important lesson that you should take from this toolkit is: "You cannot innovate alone." Likewise, The Innovation Expedition could not be written alone and without support at each stage of development. First of all, I'd like to thank all the users, facilitators and fans of the FORTH innovation method. Their ongoing support and practical feedback are what make FORTH a dynamic innovation expedition, which continues to innovate itself year after year. Next, there are a few people I'd like to thank specifically: Christine Boekholt for her excellent advice on textual content, designer Frederik de Wal for co-creating this book in a wonderful style and publisher Rudolf van Wezel for his support making The Innovation Expedition a reality. Finally, I am grateful for the internal support of my loving family. This undertaking could not have been accomplished without their boundless patience and encouragement.

Gijs van Wulfen

How to use this visual toolkit to start innovation in five steps:

1. **Innovation has got you stumped.**
2. **Read some pages.**
3. **Get inspired.**
4. **Let it incubate.**
5. **Download tools and maps and continue.**

 Download all the innovation maps and 20 practical checklists and formats to innovate the expedition way for free at www.forth-innovation.com.

Contents

This book aims to be an inspiring, visual and practical toolkit how to start innovation.
It is structured and divided into 9 sections. Inspiring maps will guide you along your innovation
expedition. As on every voyage of discovery you will be surprised. In this case inspiring quotes,
37 tools and techniques, 21 fascinating charts, 12 practical checklists and formats and 5 cases will
surprise you.

RAISE IDEAS

TEST IDEAS

HOMECOMING

I. Famous

Columbus Had to Make a Profit

In 1492 Columbus sailed off the map and assumed he had discovered a western route to the East. He named the inhabitants Indians as he was sure that he had reached the Indies. Actually he had landed at Watling Island in the Bahamas and discovered the Americas. It made him one of the most famous explorers of our times.

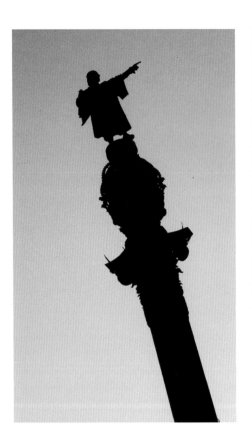

Columbus was a great navigator. Unfortunately though his estimates on the distance he needed to travel were wrong. He estimated the distance from the Canary Islands to Japan to be about 3,000 Italian miles (3,700 km or 2,300 statute miles), while in fact it was 19,600 km (12,200 miles).

Columbus left Palos de la Frontera (Spain) on August 3, 1492 with three ships: the *Nina*, the *Pinta* and the *Santa María*, carrying provisions for a year. Columbus deliberately misinformed his crew about the distances they sailed, to give them the impression of being closer to home than they actually were. After several weeks, having sailed off the map for some time, the fleet's crew began to panic. The men were terrified of never making it back home. Columbus faced a revolt only days before reaching the shore of what he believed were 'The Indies'.

Unfortunately for Columbus he did not discover a new sea route to China. Nor did he find gold on the island of *Hispaniola* (present-day Haiti and Dominican Republic). Nevertheless, returning to Castile (Spain), Queen Isabella gave Columbus all the royal titles he had demanded. Columbus persisted in his pursuit of finding a passage to the Indies by sailing west. He made four journeys; sparking Spanish colonization in the west. Meanwhile, it had become clear to everyone except Columbus himself that it wasn't the Indies that had been discovered, but a 'New World'.

So, what were the conditions that gave Columbus the courage to sail off the map?

1. Columbus came from Genoa with unclear roots and was somewhat of an outsider. He was a passionate sailor who had nothing to lose.

2. Potential profits were a strong motive. His trip was an investment and not an exploration journey. Columbus had an agreement with the monarch that if he succeeded, he would get a share of the profits from his discovery.

3. The road to the East was cut off to European traders after the fall of Constantinople to the Turks. If you wanted to seek your fortune you had to find a new route.

4. New techniques of navigation, better knowledge of the Atlantic Ocean currents and the development of the caravel made it possible to sail much closer to the wind.

5. A new era of Renaissance, which originated in Florence, encouraged new ideas.

So, if you find that small steps within your organization are not working anymore, what will it take to sail off your own map successfully?

1. Urgency. There must be urgency otherwise any innovation will be considered playtime. People are only prepared to go outside the box when there is urgency. If this is not yet the case: be patient until the conditions are right for your organization.

2. Courage. Once you feel the urgency you must follow your passion and this will carry you beyond your presumed limits. Innovate like you have nothing to lose; just like Columbus did.

3. New Technology. The development of the caravel made it possible for Columbus to sail much closer to the wind. To reach your goal you must look to experimental tools in the fields of new technology, new media and new business models.

4. Teamwork. Invite people who have a vested interest in the challenge. Also invite people for both their input on the content and in the decision-making process. This will help create internal support. The more people involved in nourishing a new idea to conception; the better the new idea will flourish.

5. Perseverance. Along the way, you can expect major setbacks. And just like Columbus and his men, there will be moments you and your team will be scared shitless. Persevere just as Columbus did before you. Sometimes what explorers first thought was a small island proved to be an enormous continent afterwards.
So, when your organization is ready; the time is right to sail off the map like Columbus did. True for any innovator: "Man cannot discover new oceans unless he has the courage to lose sight of the shore (André Gide)."

Sources
1. Wikipedia 2. David Boyle, *Voyages of Discovery*, Thames & Hudson Ltd, London, 2011. 3. Robin Hanbury-Tenison, *The Great Explorers*, Thames & Hudson ltd, London, 2010. 4. Royal Geographical Society, Alasdair Macleod, *Explorers*, Dorling Kindersley ltd, London, 2010.

HOW COLUMBUS DIS

Sources: 1. Wikipedia // 2. David Boyle, *Voyages of Discovery*, Thames & Hudson Ltd, London, 2011. //

THE EXPLORER

Christopher Columbus (c. October 31, 1451 – May 20, 1506), an explorer, navigator, and colonizer, was born in the Republic of Genoa, in what is today northwestern Italy. Under the auspices of the Catholic Monarchs of Spain, he completed four voyages across the Atlantic Ocean that led to general European awareness of the American continents.

THE CHALLENGE

Columbus's personal goal was to seek wealth by establishing a new trade route and reach the East Indies by sailing westward. He eventually received the support of the Spanish Crown, which saw in this venture a promise of gaining the upper hand over rival powers in the contest for the lucrative spice trade with Asia.

COVERED AMERICA

3. Robin Hanbury-Tenison, *The Great Explorers*, Thames & Hudson ltd, London, 2010.

THE JOURNEY

August 3, 1492, Columbus departed from Palos de la Frontera (Spain) with three ships: the *Nina*, the *Pinta* and the *Santa María*. After a stopover in Gran Canaria, it took him five weeks to cross the Atlantic Ocean. On the morning of October 12, 1492 a lookout on the *Pinta* sighted land. Columbus called the island *San Salvador* (in what is now The Bahamas). He called the inhabitants Indians being sure that he had reached the Indies.

THE SETBACKS

- Columbus incorrectly estimated the distance he needed to travel. He guessed the distance from the Canary Islands to Japan to be about 3,000 Italian miles (3,700 km, or 2,300 statute miles), while the correct figure is 19,600 km (12,200 miles).
- After several weeks and having sailed off the map, the crew was actually terrified. Columbus faced a revolt. His men were afraid that they would never be able to get back.
- The *Santa María* ran aground on Christmas Day 1492 in *Hispanolia* (present-day Haiti and the Dominican Republic) and had to be abandoned.

THE SUCCESS FACTORS

- Columbus was a bit of an outsider who had nothing to lose.
- Potential profits were a strong motive. Columbus had an agreement with the Spanish monarch that he would get a cut of the proceeds from the new lands.
- The road to the East was cut off to European traders due to the fall of Constantinople to the Turks. If you wanted to make a fortune you had to find a new route.
- New techniques of navigation, better knowledge of Atlantic currents and the development of the caravel vessel made it possible to sail much closer to the wind.
- A new era of Renaissance, which originated in Florence, encouraged new ideas.

Magellan Named the New Body of Water the Pacific Ocean for its Apparent Stillness

Ferdinand Magellan is known for his quest to find a southwest passage to the Spice Islands in the service of the King of Spain. Magellan was in fact Portuguese and in his younger years served at the Portuguese Royal court. In 1509, he served as a courageous soldier in the Spice Islands. Later however, when his service was no longer wanted by the King of Portugal, Magellan went to Spain and pledged his service to the Spanish Crown.

The Spanish were now aware that the lands of the Americas discovered by Columbus were not part of Asia, but formed a new continent. Also, the eastern routes to Asia that went around Africa were granted to Portugal in the 1494 Treaty of Tordesillas drafted by the Pope. Spain was therefore faced with an urgent need to find a new commercial route to Asia. The Spanish Crown had no other option than to explore a westward passage to the Spice Islands. Magellan

and Faleiro were named by King Charles I of Spain on March 22, 1518 as captains of a fleet to travel westward in search of these islands. The captains were promised great fame and fortune if they were successful in navigating a new route and discovering uncharted islands.
Magellan was given a fleet of five ships: the *Trinidad*, *San Antonio*, *Concepción*, *Victoria* and *Santiago* with a crew of 270 men under his command. His fleet left the Spanish harbor on September 20, 1519. Magellan could not violate the treaty with Portugal and therefore needed to avoid Brazil as it was Portuguese territory. It wasn't until October 21, 1520 that the fleet, with one ship having capsized, reached Cape Virgenes at 52°S latitude. There, they concluded that they had found the southwest passage as the salty waters ran far inland. A second ship mutinied and headed back to Spain before the fleet finished the arduous trip through the 600-kilometer long strait. This strait is known today as the Strait of Magellan. Magellan named the new body of water the *Mar Pacifico* (Pacific Ocean) for its apparent stillness.

On March 6, 1521, the remaining fleet reached the Marianas and Guam. On the morning of April 27, 1521, Magellan sailed to Mactan with a small attack force. During the resulting battle against Lapu-Lapu's troops, Magellan was hit by a bamboo spear and died from his wounds. The remaining crew of 115 men reached the Maluku Islands (the Spice Islands) on November 28, 1521. On September 6, 1522, the Spaniard Juan Sebastián Elcano and the remaining crew of Magellan's expedition arrived in Spain on the *Victoria*, almost three years after leaving the harbor.

It was not Magellan's intention to circumnavigate the world; he only intended to navigate the Spanish ships safely along a westward route to the Spice Islands. It was Elcano who, after Magellan's death, decided to push westward, thereby completing the first voyage around the entire Earth. When the *Victoria*, the last surviving ship of the fleet, returned to the Spanish harbor after circumnavigating the globe, only 18 men from the original crew of 237 men were on board.

Magellan's expedition holds four lessons for innovators:

- There was an urgent need to establish direct commercial relations between Spain and the Asian empires. That's why the expedition got the support of the King of Spain. Be sure there is demand, support and funding for your innovation expedition.

- Magellan was given unseaworthy ships and a crew of criminals. It was his tenacity that enabled Magellan to have the ships repaired and be prepared for the expedition in one and half years. Be sure that your expedition includes real innovators who share the same tenacity as Magellan.

- Magellan was able to communicate with the native tribes because his Malay interpreter could understand their languages. Be sure the members in your expedition understand new markets and speak their language before entering these new markets.

- Commercial profits from the valuable spices of the Maluku Islands were a strong motivator. The spices left on a single ship were valuable enough to pay for the entire voyage. Be sure that your innovation journey will be prosperous.

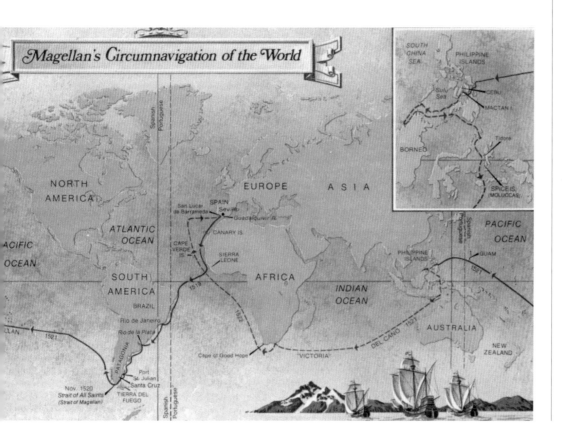

Magellan's Circumnavigation of the World

HOW MAGELLAN'S EXPEDITION

Sources: 1. Wikipedia // 2. David Boyle, *Voyages of Discovery*, Thames & Hudson Ltd, London, 2011. // 3. Robin Hanbury-Tenison, *The Great Explorers*, Thames & Hudson ltd, London, 2C

THE EXPLORER

Ferdinand Magellan (c. 1480 – April 27, 1521) was a Portuguese explorer. In the service of King Charles I of Spain, Magellan explored a westward route to the Spice Islands (in present-day Indonesia). Although it was Magellan's expedition that completed the first circumnavigation of the globe, Magellan himself was killed in the Philippines and did not complete the entire voyage.

THE CHALLENGE

The Treaty of Tordesillas in 1494 granted Portugal exclusive rights to the eastern routes around Africa. It then became imperative for Spain to establish a new commercial route to Asia. The Spanish Crown set out to discover a westward route.

THE JOURNEY

Magellan's expedition of 1519–1522 became the first expedition to sail from the Atlantic into the Pacific and to cross the Pacific Ocean. In the Philippines, Magellan took part in the Battle of Mactan. He sailed to the island with a small attack force where his men were outnumbered by natives. On the morning of April 27, 1521, Magellan was killed after being wounded by a bamboo spear. After Magellan's death, his second-in-command Elcano decided to push westward, thereby completing the first voyage around the world. On September 6, 1522, Elcano arrived in Spain aboard the *Victoria*, the last ship of the fleet, almost three years after its departure. Only 18 men from the original crew of 237 men were left on board.

THE SETBACKS

- Several problems arose during the preparation, including insufficient funding, interference from the King of Portugal and Spanish distrust of Magellan and the other Portuguese.
- On Easter 1520, there was a mutiny involving three of the five ship captains. Magellan took quick and decisive action. He had Luis de Mendoza, the captain of the *Victoria*, killed and the ship was recovered.
- During the Battle of Mactan in April 1521, Magellan was surrounded after being wounded by a bamboo spear and eventually killed.
- The casualties suffered in the Philippines left the expedition with too few men to sail the three remaining ships. The fleet was reduced to the *Trinidad* and the *Victoria*, which continued westward.
- The *Trinidad* was captured by the Portuguese and eventually wrecked in a storm.

PROVED THE WORLD IS ROUND

4. Royal Geographical Society, Alasdair Macleod, *Explorers*, Dorling Kindersley ltd, London, 2010.

THE SUCCESS FACTORS

- There was an urgent need to establish direct commercial relations between Spain and the Asian empires, without damaging relations with neighboring Portugal.
- Thanks to Magellan's skill and determination, the expedition was ready after a preparation period of one and a half years.
- Magellan was able to communicate with the native tribes because he was assisted by a Malay interpreter who could understand their languages.
- Commercial profits from the valuable spices of the Maluku Islands were a strong motivator to sail westwards and return to Spain.

André Gide,
French writer: Man cannot
oceans unless he
to lose sight

discover new
have the courage
of the shore.

As a Child Amundsen Dreamed of Being a Polar Explorer

The race for the South Pole was a big event at the beginning of the twentieth century. Roald Amundsen was described as practical, pragmatic and ruthlessly ambitious. As a child Amundsen dreamed of being a polar explorer.

Amundsen's original plan was to go to the North Pole. It was in 1909, after hearing that first Frederick Cook and then Robert Peary had claimed the North Pole for America, that Amundsen decided to reroute to Antarctica. However, he kept these plans a secret out of fear of losing funding. On June 3, 1910 Amundsen left Oslo (Norway) for the South on the *Fram*, a vessel specially designed for polar travel. In August 1910, Amundsen alerted his men at Madeira that they would be heading to Antarctica. The crew chose to stay on board. He sent a telegram to the British explorer Robert Scott, also underway to the South Pole, notifying him: "BEG TO INFORM YOU FRAM PROCEEDING ANTARCTIC

– AMUNDSEN." There is little doubt that Amundsen deliberately sought an advantage. When asked by the press for a reaction, Scott replied that his plans would not change and that he would not sacrifice the expedition's scientific goals to win the race to the Pole.

On October 19, 1911 Amundsen and four companions left his Antarctic base at the Bay of Wales on four light sleds and 52 dogs. On December 14, 1911 the team arrived at the South Pole, 33 to 34 days before Scott's group. After 99 days, Amundsen's team returned healthy and unharmed. However, on Scott's return trip to base, he and his four companions all succumbed to starvation and extreme cold.

Amundsen's expedition benefited from the simple primary focus of being first which entailed a thorough preparation, meticulous planning, knowledge of Inuit Eskimo wilderness techniques, good equipment, appropriate clothing, a skilled handling of the sled dogs and the effective use of skis. Amundsen's attention to detail is evident in the improvements he made to the boots they would wear. In his preparation, he took the boots apart; making them large enough to fit a wooden sole. The weather could drop to any temperature without the cold getting through the wooden soles and the seven pairs of stockings. Amundsen's careful preparation also included his study of innovations in snow goggles. He chose leather goggles with a slit opening for the eyes (the Bjaaland patent). They gave perfect protection and no one on the team experienced signs of snow blindness. In contrast to the tragic misfortunes of Scott's team, Amundsen's polar trek proved relatively smooth and uneventful.

THE success factor of Amundsen was preparation; the ability to foresee difficulties and take precautions to meet or avoid those difficulties.

"I may say that this is the greatest factor – the way in which the expedition is equipped – the way in which every difficulty is foreseen, and precautions taken for meeting or avoiding it. Victory awaits him who has everything in order – luck, people call it. Defeat is certain for him who has neglected to take the necessary precautions in time; this is called bad luck." –Amundsen

In comparing the achievements of Scott and Amundsen, most polar historians generally accept that Amundsen was skilled with skis and dogs, and he had a general familiarity with ice conditions, which gave him a considerable advantage in the race to the Pole. It's a wonderful source of inspiration for innovators. It has everything to do with preparation. So, you better choose the right innovation challenge at the right moment with the right team going on the right track with the right equipment and the right support. You can only start an innovation project once for the first time.

HOW AMUNDSEN REACHED

Sources: 1. Wikipedia // 2. Robin Hanbury-Tenison, *The Great Explorers*, Thames & Hudson ltd, London, 2010. //

THE EXPLORER

Roald Amundsen (July 16, 1872 – c. June 18, 1928) was a Norwegian explorer of Polar Regions. He led the Antarctic expedition (1910-1912) to reach the center of the South Pole in December 1911.

THE CHALLENGE

The race for the Poles was a big event at the beginning of the twentieth century. Amundsen had made plans to go to the North Pole. In 1909, after hearing that first Frederick Cook and then Robert Peary had claimed the North Pole for America, Amundsen decided to reroute to Antarctica. He sent a telegram to the British explorer Robert Scott, also under-way to the South Pole, notifying him: "BEG TO INFORM YOU FRAM PROCEEDING ANTARCTIC – AMUNDSEN."

THE JOURNEY

On October 19, 1911, Amundsen and four companions left their Antarctic base at the Bay of Wales on four light sleds and 52 dogs. On December 14, 1911, the team arrived at the South Pole, 33 to 34 days before Robert Scott's group. After 99 days, Amundsen's team returned healthy and unharmed.

THE SOUTH POLE FIRST

3. Royal Geographical Society, Alasdair Macleod, *Explorers*, Dorling Kindersley ltd, London, 2010. // 4. Roald Amundsen, *The South Pole*, Cooper Square Press, New York, 2001.

THE SETBACK

Amundsen's original plan was to go to the North Pole. It was in 1909, after hearing that first Frederick Cook and then Robert Peary had claimed the North Pole for America, that Amundsen decided to reroute to Antarctica.

THE SUCCESS FACTORS

- Flexibility.
- The simple primary focus of being first.
- Thorough preparation.
- Meticulous planning.
- Knowledge of Inuit Eskimo wilderness techniques.
- Good equipment.
- Appropriate clothing.
- Skilled handling of sled dogs.
- The effective use of skis.

"Well George, we Knocked the Bastard Off."

These were the first words of Edmund Hillary to his old friend George Low meeting him near the South Col of Mount Everest. It was just after his historic climb with his Nepalese Sherpa Tenzing Norgay on May 29, 1953. George welcomed Hillary with hot tomato soup from a thermos flask. Hillary and Norgay were the first ones confirmed to have reached the summit of Mount Everest. Hillary's book View from the Summit describes his adventures in detail.

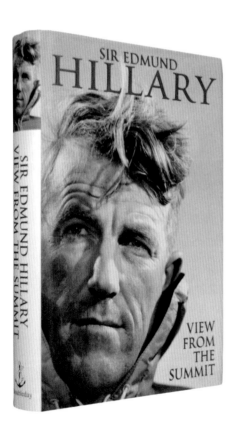

In the fifties, the route to Everest was closed by Chinese-controlled Tibet. Nepal only allowed one expedition per year. Hillary had been part of a British reconnaissance expedition to the mountain two years earlier in 1951. The 1953 Everest expedition consisted of a huge team of over 400 people, including 362 porters, 20 Sherpa guides and almost 5,000 kilograms of baggage. Expedition leader Hunt named two British mountaineers: Tom Bourdillon and Charles Evans as the first assault team. Hillary and Norgay were the second assault team. Bourdillon and Evans attempted the climb, but due to a failing oxygen system only reached the South Col, about 100 meters below the summit. Then Hillary and Norgay got their chance. A crucial last part of climbing Mount Everest is a 12-meter rock face, which Hillary managed to climb. Today it is known as the Hillary Step. They reached the 8,848-meter high summit, the highest point on Earth, at 11:30 a.m. on May 29, 1953.

Reaching the highest point on Earth is one of the greatest expeditions of mankind. It made Hillary famous. Reading Hillary's View from the Summit, ten elements of innovation occurred to me on being first.

1. Passion. As a youngster, Hillary was a great dreamer. He read many adventure books and walked many miles with his head in the clouds. He was unaware his passion for adventure would make him, together with Tenzing Norgay, the first man to set foot on the highest point on Earth.

2. Urgency. In 1952 the British heard that the French had been given permission to attempt Everest in 1954. The British wanted more than anything to be first. The expedition just had to succeed.

3. Teamwork. Getting to the summit of Everest is all about teamwork. As Hillary wrote: "John Hunt and D Namgyal's lift to the depot on the South-East Ridge; George Low, Alf Gregory and Ang Nyima with their superb support at Camp

IX; and the pioneer effort by Charles Evans and Tom Bourdillon to the South Summit. Their contribution had enabled us to make such good progress."

4. Courage. The Khumbu Icefall is the first major hurdle to cross at Everest. It is vast and unstable, and has claimed more lives than any other part of the South-East approach. The higher you get on Everest the more courage you need. At 7,800 meters Hillary wrote in his diary: "Even wearing all my down clothing I found the icy breath from outside penetrating through my bones. A terrible sense of fear and loneliness dominated my thoughts. What is the sense of this all? I asked myself."

5. Test. On the 1951 reconnaissance expedition, team members tested oxygen equipment and did research on high-altitude physiology. The results of both studies were important in determining the right approach for Everest in 1953.

6. Initiative. While in India, Hillary read in a newspaper that the British were taking an expedition to the south side of Mount Everest in 1951. He wrote a letter to expedition leader Eric Shipton suggesting that a couple of members of a New Zealand climbing expedition could make a substantial contribution to the team. And so two New Zealanders were invited. If you want something you have to take the initiative.

7. Choices. The British Himalayan Committee replaced the 1951 expedition leader Eric Shipton with Colonel John Hunt, a climber. After eight failed attempts on Everest they needed someone to the top first, before the French would have their chance.

8. Overcome setbacks. Along the way there are always major setbacks. After finding a new route up Everest during the reconnaissance expedition of 1951, the British heard that the Swiss had obtained permission for two attempts on Everest the following year. The only thing the British could do was wait and see if the Swiss would succeed.

9. Competition. Who would be the top teams? And which of them would get the first chance? That was the question. Hunt proposed that Evans and Bourdillon should use the closed-circuit oxygen equipment to reach the South Summit and Norgay and Hillary would push to the top with the open-circuit oxygen. Hillary describes the terms first and second assault team as completely misleading.

10. Luck. With so many possible setbacks you also need some luck. First of all, Hillary, a New Zealander, was lucky to qualify as a British subject and be invited to join the British team. The second bit of luck was in 1952 when the Swiss failed to climb Everest on their two attempts. In their first attempt, the Swiss climbed Everest just 300 meters below the summit before they had to retreat due to utter exhaustion. In autumn 1952, their second attempt ended just above the South Col due to low temperatures and strong winds, leaving Everest unclimbed.
Hillary was the first confirmed to have reached the summit of Mount Everest. It changed his life. May his story inspire you to follow your passion and realize your innovation dreams.

HOW HILLARY AND TENZING

Sourcess: 1. Wikipedia // 2. Sir Edmund Hillary, *View from the Summit*, Simon & Schuster, New York, 2000.

THE EXPLORERS

Sir Edmund Percival Hillary (July 20, 1919 – January 20, 2008) was a New Zealand mountaineer, explorer and philanthropist. Tenzing Norgay (late May 1914 – May 9, 1986) was a Nepalese Indian Sherpa mountaineer. On May 29, 1953, Hillary and Tenzing became the first climbers confirmed as having reached the summit of Mount Everest.

THE CHALLENGE

Mount Everest is Earth's highest mountain, with a peak at 8,848 meters (29,029 ft) above sea level. In the fifties, the route to Everest was closed by Chinese-controlled Tibet. Nepal only allowed one expedition per year. In 1952 the British heard that the French had been given permission to attempt Everest in 1954. After eight failed attempts on Everest, the British just had to be first to succeed.

THE JOURNEY

The 1953 Everest expedition consisted of a huge team of over 400 people, including 362 porters, 20 Sherpa guides and almost 5,000 kilograms of baggage. Hillary and Norgay were the second assault team. They reached the summit, the highest point on Earth, at 11:30 am on May 29, 1953.

CLIMBED MOUNT EVEREST

THE SETBACKS

- After the reconnaissance expedition of 1951, the British heard that the Swiss had obtained permission for two attempts on Everest the following year. The only thing left to do was wait and see if the Swiss would succeed.
- The Khumbu Icefall is the first major hurdle to cross at Everest. It is vast and unstable, and has claimed more lives than any other part of the South-East approach.
- The first of the two climbing teams to attempt to reach the summit, Tom Bourdillon and Charles Evans, came within 100 meters of the summit on May 29, 1953, but turned back after encountering problems with their oxygen equipment.

- From the South Summit at the end of a traverse at 8,760 meters is an imposing 12-meter rock wall now called the *Hillary Step*. Hillary and Tenzing were the first climbers to ascend this step with primitive ice climbing equipment and ropes.

THE SUCCESS FACTORS

- In 1952 the British heard that the French had been given permission to attempt Everest in 1954. The British expedition could not fail again in 1953. They just had to be first to succeed.
- The British Himalayan Committee replaced the 1951 expedition leader Eric Shipton with a climber named Colonel John Hunt.
- On the 1951 reconnaissance expedition, team members tested oxygen equipment and did research on high-altitude physiology. The results of both studies were important in deciding on the right approach for Everest in 1953.
- As anticipated, work previously done by the first climbing pair in route finding, breaking trail and testing storage of extra oxygen were all of great aid to Hillary and Tenzing.

President JFK Had to Restore America's Prestige

"I think we're going to the Moon because it's in the nature of human being to face challenges. It's by the nature of his deep inner soul. We're required to do these things just as salmon swim upstream." (Neil Armstrong)

Neil Armstrong was a calm, quiet and self-confident man. It wasn't in his nature to seek the spotlight. He learned to fly in the summer of 1946 at the age of sixteen. This was the minimum age to fly a powered airplane. It was rather unusual that he earned his pilot's license before getting his driver's license. Flying was his passion. He resented the fact that all the record-setting flights over the ocean were already accomplished.

In 1957 the Soviet Union launched Sputnik, the world's first satellite, into orbit. This event created urgency in the United States. The Americans prioritized their Mercury program, which aimed to launch a man into space. On April 12, 1961 the Soviet Union stunned the world again when cosmonaut Yuri Gagarin became the first man in space. President JFK had to restore America's prestige and wanted to show American superiority. He declared "I believe that this entire nation should commit itself to achieving the goal, before the decade is out, of landing a man on the Moon and returning him safely to Earth." Armstrong's application for astronaut selection in the Mercury program in 1962 missed the June 1st deadline by a week. But a former flight simulation specialist saw to it that Armstrong's application made it into the pile prior to the selection panel's first meeting.

In 1965 Armstrong was named back-up commander on *Gemini V*. Each flight crew had a back-up crew. In some flights it turned out that members of the back-up crew had to step in. Three and a half years into his career as an astronaut, Neil Armstrong made his first space shot on *Gemini VIII*. When former navy aviator colleagues heard Armstrong had been selected for the first Moon landing on *Apollo 11* they described it as "luck, opportunity, preparation and skill converged".

After a decade of preparation it almost went wrong at the last moment. In the descent to the Moon suddenly a yellow caution light came on: '1202 program alarm'. Armstrong did not know which of the dozen of alarms it represented. Mission Control said it was not critical and the mission continued.
Landing on the moon is one of the greatest explorations of mankind thus far. While learning how Kennedy landed the first man on the moon, seven innovation lessons popped into my head.

1. Urgency. President JFK had to restore America's prestige and wanted to exert a show of American superiority over the Soviets. The honor of a whole nation was at stake. Therefore time and money were dedicated to the space program and everyone involved was prepared to think and act outside the box.

2. Challenge. Start your innovation journey with a clear and impressive challenge. In this case it was a very clear assignment: before the decade is out, land a man on the Moon.

3. Focus. During your innovation journey, a concrete assignment serves as a guide to make the right decisions. There were three theoretical options for landing on the Moon: Direct Ascent, Earth Orbit Rendezvous and Lunar Orbit Rendezvous (LOR). In July 1962, to the surprise of many experts, NASA opted for the Lunar Orbit Rendezvous. If the Rendezvous failed the astronauts would be too far away to be saved. The most important factor was that LOR was the only way to have a Moon landing by the end of the decade and meet Kennedy's deadline.

4. Prepare. On the morning of the launch, the first astronaut on board the Apollo 11 was not one of the regular crew: Armstrong, Collins or Aldrin. It was Fred Haise, Aldrin's back-up as lunar module pilot. Haise ran through a 417-step checklist designed to ensure that every switch was set in the proper position. Be sure to have your own '417-step checklist'.

5. Test. The *Apollo 10* was a full-dress rehearsal for *Apollo 11*. They flew almost precisely the same track over the lunar surface that Apollo 11 would be flying. They took pictures of the descent and landing areas. This was very helpful according to Neil Armstrong: "By the time we launched in July, we knew all the principal landmarks on our descent path by heart." So test, test and test.

6. Teamwork. "Within the flight crews we divided the responsibilities such that each would go into their area in substantially more depth." Innovate as a team and you get better results as well as greater internal support for the outcome.

7. Passion. At age 16, Neil Armstrong got his pilot's license before getting his driver's license. Flying was his real passion. Follow your passion in your innovation projects. And only do things on your own terms.

The dark side of the Moon for Neil Armstrong personally was becoming the most famous man on Earth overnight. He remained a very modest man, stating to his biographer in 2004: "I think people should be recognized for their achievements and the value that adds to society's progress. But it can be easily overdone. I think highly of many people and their accomplishments, but I don't believe that should be paramount over the actual achievements themselves. Celebrity shouldn't supersede the things they've accomplished."

Neil Armstrong was a great man.

Source:
James R. Hanssen,
'First Man, the
Life of Neil
A. Armstrong',
Simon & Schuster,
New York, 2005.

HOW ARMSTRONG SET

THE EXPLORER

Neil Armstrong (August 5, 1930 – August 25, 2012) was an American astronaut and the first person to set foot on the Moon. Armstrong's second and last spaceflight was the moon landing in July 1969 as mission commander of Apollo 11.

THE CHALLENGE

On April 12, 1961 the Soviet Union stunned the world when cosmonaut Yuri Gagarin became the first man in space. President John F. Kennedy had to restore America's respect and wanted to show American superiority. He declared: "I believe that this entire nation should commit itself to achieving the goal, before the decade is out, of landing a man on the Moon and returning him safely to Earth."

THE JOURNEY

The Apollo program was the third human spaceflight program carried out by NASA, the U.S. civil space agency. The Apollo program was dedicated to President John F. Kennedy's national goal. The crew of Apollo 8 sent the first live televised pictures of Earth and the Moon back to Earth on Christmas Eve 1968. This is believed to be the most widely watched television broadcast up until that time. By the end of the 1960s Kennedy's goal was accomplished by the Apollo 11 mission. Astronauts Neil Armstrong and Buzz Aldrin landed the Apollo Lunar Module on the Moon on July 20, 1969 and walked on its surface. The final cost of the Apollo program was reported to Congress as $25.4 billion in 1973.

FOOT ON THE MOON

Sources: 1. Wikipedia // 2. James R. Hanssen, 'First Man, the Life of Neil A. Armstrong', Simon & Schuster, New York, 2005.

THE SETBACKS

- The major setback in the Apollo program was the 1967 Apollo 1 cabin fire that killed the entire crew during a pre-launch test.
- It was suspenseful up until the final moments before the first landing. During the descent to the Moon a yellow caution light suddenly came on: *'1202 program alarm'*. Mission Control said it was not critical and the mission continued.

THE SUCCESS FACTORS

- Urgency. President JFK had to restore America's respect and wanted to show American superiority over the Soviets. The honor of an entire nation was at stake.
- Focus. The immense goal served as a guide to make the right decisions.
- Test. Everything was tested and retested. The Apollo 10 was a full-dress rehearsal for Apollo 11.
- Teamwork. "Within the flight crews we divided the responsibilities such that each would go into their area in substantially more depth." Each flight crew also had a back-up crew.

WHY DO EXPEDITIONS

5. Equipment malfunctions. In April of 1970, Apollo 13 was launched. The third manned lunar mission was aborted when a short circuit caused an oxygen tank to explode. The ship managed to hold together as it passed the dark side of the Moon and limped back to Earth. The fact that there was no loss of life is a testament to the courage and skill of the astronauts and the ground support team.

1. Killed by the cold. John Franklin set out in 1845 in pursuit of the legendary Northwest Passage, a navigable sea lane above North America. The problem that Franklin faced was that the Northwest Passage is ice-locked almost year-round. In 1846, when Franklin's expedition became stuck in the ice, it was only a matter of time before the cold and starvation claimed the lives of Franklin's entire crew.

2. Killed by the crew. Charles Francis Hall was an experienced Arctic explorer who had been on two previous expeditions. In June 1871 he set out on an expedition to the North Pole. He died on his ship in November in what is now called Hall Bay. Later investigation determined that he had ingested large amounts of arsenic and was likely poisoned by his crew. His second-in-command, Sidney Budington took over the expedition and despite reaching a record latitude also failed to reach the Pole.

3. Ill-prepared. Three Swedes: S.A. Andree and his crew Nils Strindberg and Knut Fraenkel set out for the North Pole in a hydrogen balloon in 1897, crashed and later perished in the Arctic. "... You had three guys with desk jobs from Stockholm who hadn't done a whole lot of preparation." Their ropes got tangled up and lost. Unable to steer, they eventually sailed over the horizon.

4. Overcrowded. In the spring of 1996 a group of inexperienced adventure seekers and their well-paid guides of the IMAX expedition set out to conquer Mount Everest. Overcrowding and weather led to the deaths of 12 climbers, including some of the very experienced guides. Following the tragic expedition, some controversy was raised about the irresponsibility of promoting commercial tours to novice climbers to ascent Earth's highest summit, Mount Everest.

6. Starvation. In April of 1846, George and Jacob Donner decided it was time to head out west from Illinois to California. Together with several other families they were swayed by promises of a shorter and easier trail. In reality, it turned out to be a longer and harder trail. The Donner party arrived at the Sierra Nevada mountain range after winter conditions set in and blocked the pass. Of the 90 original members in the Donner party, 48 survived to see California.

7. Poor leadership. In the late 1690s, William Paterson figured he could make Scotland a world trading nation by establishing a colony called "New Caledonia" on the Isthmus of Panama. Paterson's expedition loaded 5 ships that carried 1200 people. The ships made landfall off the coast of Darien (Panama) on November 2, 1698. What followed was the result of poor planning compounded by evener poorer leadership. First they constructed a fort in an

FAIL?

area without a fresh water supply. Then they set up fields to grow maize and yams, which no one knew how to cultivate. Nor did the settlers know how to store food in the heat and humidity of Panama. The death rate rose to 10 settlers a day.

8. Storm. In 1527, a crew of five ships and 600 men under the command of Pánfilo de Narváez made their way to the New World from Spain. They were sailing along, doing pretty well, when a hurricane struck their fleet in the Gulf of Mexico. In April of 1528, de Narváez and the remaining 300 men landed near the Rio de las Palmas among hostile natives. Thinking they were near Mexico, his expedition marched northward through interior Florida until it reached the territory of the powerful Apalachee Indians. Narváez decided to cut his losses and get the hell out. He ordered the construction of four rafts to return to the sea from the interior. He intended to rejoin the ships and continue to Mexico,

but the vessels were destroyed in yet another storm. Narváez and almost all the members of his expedition died. • • • • •

9. Inexperience. In 1860, the government of Australia put out a reward of 2000 pounds to anyone who succeeded in crossing the North-South interior of the continent. An expedition was led by a man named Robert Burke, a former police superintendant, with absolutely no experience in bushcraft. On August 21, 1860 with much fanfare, Burke's group headed out of Melbourne with 19 men, 23 horses, 6 wagons and 26 camels. Who knows what he was thinking when he decided to pack a handy cedar-topped oak camp table, chairs, rockets, flags… and of course, a Chinese gong. Burke clearly lacked experience in preparing for this ill-fated expedition. In fact, the equipment and food in total weighed some 20 tons causing one wagon to break down even before leaving Royal Park. The expedition was so heavily

weighed down that by midnight they had only gotten as far as the edges of Melbourne.

10. Flawed design. In 1967, the space race was in full swing and the Soviets had not put a man in space for over two years. The *Soyuz 1* was designed to launch cosmonaut Vladimir Komarov into space. Before returning to Earth, Komarov would meet with *Soyuz 2*, which was scheduled to be launched the next day. However, *Soyuz 1* experienced failures in space with the solar panel and stabilization mechanism. The mission of *Soyuz 2* was altered to include repairing *Soyuz 1*. Tragically, thunderstorms prevented the launch of *Soyuz 2* and *Soyuz 1* had to re-enter the atmosphere unrepaired. Failure of the main parachute and entanglement of the reserve chute led to an explosive impact causing the death of Komarov. Prior to launching the ill-fated *Soyuz 1*, test flights had been plagued with failures with over 200 design flaws documented by engineers; and yet the mission still went ahead.

Sources: www.timetoeatthedogs.com, www.pbs.org/franklin-expedition, www.npr.org, www.totallytop10.com/history/top-10-doomed-expeditions, www.ranker.com/list/10-of-the-most-doomed-expeditions-in-history/, www.brainz.org/10-scientific-expeditions-were-doomed-start/.

Aldous Huxley,
English writer:

To travel is everyone other

to discover that is wrong about countries.

10 Innovation Lessons from Great Explorers

"Men wanted for hazardous journey. Small wages, bitter cold, long months of complete darkness, constant danger and safe return doubtful. Honour and recognition in case of success."

MEN WANTED FOR HAZARDOUS JOURNEY. SMALL WAGES, BITTER COLD, LONG MONTHS OF COMPLETE DARKNESS, CONSTANT DANGER AND SAFE RETURN DOUBTFUL. HONOUR AND RECOGNITION IN CASE OF SUCCESS

This advertisement ran in a London newspaper in 1913. Could you have imagined answering it? If so, you are a real innovator. Just like you, over 1000 men did. They were hoping to be chosen for an Antarctic polar expedition led by Sir Ernest Shackleton. He gained fame for his 1909 expedition to the South Pole. When I read this ad in one of my travel books it struck me that 100 years later this could have been an ad for an innovation project. Modern day innovation has striking similarities with historic voyages of discovery.

A promised land

Most people searched for adventure only when it was really necessary and when they had nothing to lose. This was true for Columbus and Magellan, both having left their country of origin. Likewise, with the world changing at a faster pace, organizations are facing changing markets. They begin to feel real urgency the moment their 'old solutions' stop working and they start looking for a new promised land.

The challenge of being first

On April 12, 1961 the Soviet Union stunned the world when cosmonaut Yuri Gagarin became the first man in space. President John F. Kennedy had to restore America's respect and wanted to show American superiority. He declared:

"I believe that this entire nation should commit itself to achieving the goal, before the decade is out, of landing a man on the Moon and returning him safely to Earth." All explorers strive to be first. Amundsen reaching the South Pole, Livingstone searching for the source of the Nile, Hillary climbing Mount Everest. Entrepreneurs share the same ambition: developing 'new-to-the-world' innovations to outsmart the competition.

A group effort

Explorers rarely go alone. Columbus sailed to America with a crew of ninety men on three ships. Hillary could not have conquered Everest if Tenzing Norgay hadn't first saved him from a fall into a crevasse. Amundsen traveled light with four companions to be first at the South Pole. Each flight crew in the Apollo program had back-up crew members; some of whom as it turned out had to step in. Within complex organizations you cannot innovate alone either. You need people from every discipline to develop a new product, produce it, market it, sell it, bill it and service it.

A long journey

Discovery voyages lasted many years due to unexpected setbacks brought on by an unknown illness, a tropical storm or mutiny by the crew. The first circumnavigation of the Earth by Magellan and Elcano in 1522 took more than three years, after preparing their trip for one and a half years. It took the Americans eight years to get Neil Armstrong on the Moon after Kennedy's speech on May 5, 1961. The average time for the development process of a new product takes about 18 to 36 months from concept to introduction and follows similar patterns.

High risk of no return

Many ships may perish along the way. On Magellan's circumnavigation of the Earth, four of his five ships did not return. Magellan, himself, was fatally wounded while under attack in the Pacific. Nevertheless, the cargo of the last remaining ship, the *Victoria*, made the whole expedition worthwhile. It's similar in innovation. Six of every seven newly developed product ideas perish along the way. Of the seven, only one product enters the market successfully.

Serendipity

Serendipity leads to greater rewards. Sometimes what explorers first thought was a small island proved to be an enormous continent afterwards. As the Vikings did who had discovered North America long before Columbus. Compare this with the development of SMS services. It was originally developed for the B2B market, but it did not catch on. After young people caught on to the idea of SMS as a cheap way to contact each other, it became a worldwide market with more than three billion users. Having so many similarities to voyages of discovery, what practical lessons are there for innovators inspired by successful explorers?

1. Passion. At age 16, Neil Armstrong got his pilot's license before getting his driver's license. Flying was his real passion. Follow your passion in your innovation projects. And only do things on your own terms. This will give you confidence and courage to land your innovation project safely, even when some non-critical alarm keeps going off.

2. Urgency. This creates momentum for your innovation project. In the 1494 Treaty of Tordesillas, drafted by the Pope, the eastern sea routes that went along Africa to the Spice Islands were reserved for Portugal. It was urgent for Spain to find a new route to the west. In absence of urgency or a promised land, innovation is considered as playtime and nobody will be prepared to go outside the box. Be patient until your organization is ready.

3. Challenge. It is needed to start your innovation journey. In 1952 the British heard that the French had been given permission to attempt Everest in 1954.

The British wanted more than anything to be first. The expedition just had to succeed.

4. Teamwork. Neil Armstrong stated "Within the flight crews we divided the responsibilities such that each would go into their area in substantially more depth." Teamwork will get you better results and greater support for the outcome.

5. Plan. The Apollo program, the route of Hillary and Tenzing to the summit of Mount Everest and the route of Amundsen to the South Pole. All were meticulously planned. So plan your project in a structured way step by step.

6. Preparation. Amundsen's success factor was preparation. As he, himself, stated: "I may say that this is the greatest factor – the way in which the expedition is equipped – the way in which every difficulty is foreseen, and precautions taken for meeting or avoiding it. Victory awaits him who has everything in order." Another example of careful preparation is the Apollo program. On the morning of the launch, the first astronaut on board the Apollo 11 was not one of the regular crew: Armstrong, Collins or Aldrin. It was Fred Haise, Aldrin's back-up as lunar module pilot. Haise ran through a 417-step checklist designed to ensure

that every switch was set to the proper position. Be sure to have your own '417-step checklist'.

7. Focus. During your innovation journey, a concrete mission serves as a guide to make the right decisions. There were three theoretical options for landing on the Moon: Direct Ascent, Earth Orbit Rendezvous and Lunar Orbit Rendezvous (LOR). In July 1962, to the surprise of many experts, NASA opted for the Lunar Orbit Rendezvous. If the Rendezvous failed the astronauts would be too far away to be saved. The most important factor in the decision was that LOR was the only way to have a Moon landing by the end of the decade and meet Kennedy's deadline. So, keep your focus to maintain speed and shorten marketing time.

8. Perseverance. Magellan was an outsider. He was a Portuguese navigator leading a fleet of Spanish ships. He had nothing to lose. He was given unseaworthy ships and a crew of criminals. It took him one and a half years to repair the ships and prepare for the expedition. The tenacity of Magellan is a character trait of real innovators. The last remaining ship of his fleet completed the first circumnavigation of the Earth three years after leaving harbor.

9. New technology. The development of the caravel made it possible for Columbus to sail much closer to the wind. Amundsen benefited from well-designed boots and innovations in snow goggles for better protection on the South Pole. Look to experimental tools in the fields of new technology, new media and new business models to reach your goal.

10. Empathy. Magellan was able to communicate with the native tribes because his Malay interpreter could understand their languages. Amundsen's familiarity with ice conditions, gave him a considerable advantage in the race to the South Pole. He had acquired knowledge from Inuit Eskimos as to their wilderness techniques. Be sure you understand new markets and speak their language before you enter those markets. Unfortunately, Shackleton's Trans-Antarctic expedition was not a success. His ship the *Endurance* was destroyed by Arctic ice. Nevertheless it ended "all safe, all well." Shackleton was able to rescue his crew of 22 men on Elephant Island. Even if you cannot overcome all innovation pitfalls and you fail to reach your goal, remember to bring your team back safely and learn from your joint effort. In innovation the journey itself is as vital as the end result.

10 INNOVATION LESSONS

Ten practical innovation lessons inspired by successful explorers like Christopher Columbus, Ferdinand Magellan, Roald Amundsen, Edmund Hillary, and Neil Armstrong.

10 INNOVATION LESSONS

1. PASSION — It will give you confidence and the courage to proceed.

2. URGENCY — It will create momentum for your innovation project.

3. CHALLENGE — It will serve as a guide during your innovation journey.

4. TEAMWORK — It will lead to better results and greater support.

5. PLAN — It will support your leadership and give confidence.

6. PREPARATION — *Victory awaits him who has everything in order.* (Roald Amundsen).

7. FOCUS — It will maintain speed and shorten the time to market.

8. PERSEVERANCE — It will take you to where no man has gone before.

9. NEW TECHNOLOGY — It will make your new solution feasible.

10. EMPATHY — It will provide you with relevant customer insights.

II.

Innovate the

Expedition
Way

21 Situations When You Should Not Innovate

Innovation can either be 'doing things differently' or 'doing different things'. There's currently a lot going on in the field of innovation, like *'Sustainable Innovation', 'Business Model Innovation', 'Service innovation', 'Collaborative Innovation', 'Participatory Innovation', 'Social Innovation', 'Employee Driven Innovation', 'Brand Driven Innovation', 'Agile Innovation'* and *'Frugal Innovation'*.

You might get the impression that innovation is the right management tool at any moment for any and every market or organization. Well, in my opinion it´s not. To illustrate, let's take a look at historical expeditions and why many of them failed. Expeditions that never succeeded due to the cold, heavy storms or starvation. Expeditions like that of John Franklin, whose entire fleet perished while looking for the legendary Northwest Passage in 1845. Or those who were inexperienced like Andrée who set out for the North Pole in a hydrogen balloon in 1897. Or expeditions that suffered from design faults and equipment malfunctions like the *Soyuz 1* in 1967 or *Apollo 13* in 1970. Or expeditions that lacked the right leadership and team spirit like the expedition leader Charles Francis Hall who was poisoned by his crew in 1871 on a Polar expedition.

Drawing from the learning experiences of both successful as well as failed expeditions, I have compiled a list of 21 situations when you should not innovate. I am aware that this can be provoking. It's meant to be. This is where innovation starts: opening people's minds, challenging current opinions, habits and practices.

21 Situations when you should not innovate:

1. When you are sure your market is not changing in the coming five years.
2. When your clients are even more conservative than you are.
3. When your old formulas are still giving great risk-free results for the coming years.
4. When brand and line extensions bring you a lot of extra turnover and profits.
5. When the urgency to innovate is completely absent.
6. When you don't receive enough money and manpower to do it.
7. When your company is in a short-term crisis.
8. When your organization is working at full capacity to meet the current huge demand.
9. When everybody says: "Innovate!", but no one wants to be responsible.
10. When you´re clueless about what you´re looking for.
11. When there is no real business need and it's only nice to have.
12. When you can't form a capable harmonious team that really goes for it.
13. When there is no support at the top.
14. When the people in your organization are not (yet) prepared to break their habits.
15. When people in your company are lazy; content to copy from others.
16. When the organization doesn't have any kind of vision about its future course.
17. When long term planning means looking three months ahead.
18. When everyone fears failure.
19. When everyone will attack and ridicule the newness of an idea.
20. When important stakeholders will block it at any time.
21. When your latest innovations are so successful and still need further exploitation.

So, what *is* the moment to innovate? Well that's when you don't recognize any of the circumstances above. Be aware though. I learned as a young manager that you can invent alone, but in an organization you cannot innovate alone.

You need an awful lot of colleagues and bosses to make innovation happen. That's because after the ideation of your product, you'll need to design it, to develop it, to prototype it, to test it, to produce it, to sell it, to invoice it and to service it. So, keeping these situations in mind; remember to wait for the right moment, as you'll only have one chance to start innovation for the first time.

6 Ways of Committing Innovation Suicide

Customers change. Competitors change. Technology changes. If you don't do anything; new, competitive products and services will catch up and overtake your products and services. A study by Arthur D. Little has shown that the life cycle of products has shrunk by an average of 400 percent over the last fifty years'. Innovation, therefore, is essential.

When starting innovation, a lot of the same mistakes are made over and over again. That's why you need to be aware of these six ways of committing innovation suicide. And how to avoid these pitfalls in practice.

1. Start without a business need.
Think about the last time you tried to make a dramatic change in your personal behavior. We, as innovators, are faced with the same difficulties. We are all stuck in our habits; doing things in fixed patterns. For years, we continue to read the same journals, drive the same cars, and have the same insurance. The only reason for us to change is when a new, simple and attractive solution comes along, relevant to our needs. It's as simple as that. So, if your company's current business is booming; it's unlikely that the people in your organization will readily break with their habits. Remember: necessity is the mother of invention. The 1494 Treaty of Tordesillas granted Portugal exclusive rights to the eastern routes that went along Africa. That's why on March 22, 1518 the King of Spain was persuaded to appoint Magellan and Faleiro joint captains; the Spanish Crown felt an urgent need to travel west to find a new commercial route to the Spice Islands. So, don't try to convince others to innovate when there is no business need; you will be turned down.

2. To first appoint an innovator.
Okay, we need to innovate, so who do we put in charge? A lot of organizations will make the most innovative colleague responsible for innovation. That may seem like the smart thing to do, but it's not. He or she will only end up a lone wolf, because inventing and innovating are two very different things. You can invent on your own. But in an organization you can never innovate alone! You need R&D engineers, production managers, IT staff, financial controllers, marketers, service people and salesmen to develop or service the product, produce it and get it on the market. The moment you appoint an innovator, you run the risk that everyone else will lean back and wait for the appointed innovator to come up with his or her innovations. The others won't take their responsibility anymore.

3. Start with your idea.
Innovation isn't just about ideas; it's about getting the right ones and realizing these ideas in practice. The global symbol for innovation is a bright, shining light bulb. Once an idea comes to you, you'll probably fall in love with it. That's a great feeling. But, unfortunately, love is blind. The psychological phenomenon of selective perception will make you see only the positive points of an idea and only listen to people who are supportive. What happens when you tell your idea to someone else? The first reaction will often be 'Yes, but…' Others within your group will be critical of your idea the moment it is told to them. An important reason for this is that it is your idea and not theirs.

4. Bet on one idea.

For every seven ideas for a new product, about 4 enter development, 1 to 2 are launched and only 1 succeeds.[2] It resembles the outcome of Magellan's expedition. On September 20, 1519 five ships under Magellan's command – *Trinidad, San Antonio, Concepción, Victoria* and *Santiago* – left Spain to discover a route to the west. Three years later only one ship, the *Victoria*, returned to the harbor of departure, completing the first circumnavigation of the Earth. However, the spices on the *Victoria*, were so valuable, it was enough to pay for the entire expedition. Therefore, never bet on one ship. There's a huge risk that it won't return.

5. Start with a brainstorming session.

When there's a need to come up with something new, people generally start by organizing a brainstorming session. Ironically, often times nothing innovative ever materializes. That's why brainstorming holds such negative connotations in lots of companies. It's because it is usually the same group of colleagues who get together to brainstorm without any preparation. You might think the problem is their inability to generate new ideas. But you would be wrong. The problem is their inability to let go of the old ones! I love this quote by the American businessman Dee Hock, he says: "The problem is never how to get new, innovative thoughts into your mind, but how to get old ones out. Every mind is a building filled with archaic furniture. Clean out a corner of your mind and creativity will instantly fill it. Once you get the old ideas out of your mind, new ones come automatically!"

6. Start by neglecting customers.

Starting with ideas or new technologies gives a lot of energy and inspiration. It's also fun to do. But effective innovation is all about getting new ideas for simple solutions for relevant customer problems or needs. Meeting potential customers to discover their frictions belongs to a set of highly effective techniques you want to apply when creating new product ideas. Robert Cooper and Scott Edgett confirm this in their study concerning ideation techniques.[3] Don't go looking for what your customer wants. This is because customers, themselves, aren't always able to articulate their needs. Start by exploring customers' relevant future problems. You'll soon find that neglecting customers in your innovation will lead to a dead-end street for sure.

1. Source: A.D. Little as cited in C.F. von Braun 'The Innovation War' (Upper Saddle River. N.J.: Prentice Hall PTR, 1997).
2. R. Cooper (2005), Product Leadership. New York: Basic Books.
3. R. Cooper & S. Edgett (March 2008), "Ideation for Product Innovation: What are the Best Methods?" PDMA Visions.

40 REASONS WHY PEOPLE **STRUGGLE**

CULTURE

UNCERTAINTY

SUPPORT

1. Are we creative?
2. How do we change our habits?
3. We don't dare to think innovative.
4. We are lazy.
5. We lack curiosity.
6. We are not aware of the need.
7. We don't believe innovation is going to happen.
8. We have always done it this way.
9. We do not have the guts.
10. Our failures blocks new initiatives.
11. We have a short-term mindset.
12. We don't have a vision.

13. When do we have to start?
14. Our ideas seem unfeasible.
15. We find it hard to imagine the future.
16. We fear failure.
17. Others will ridicule us.
18. We don't know if it leads to profits.

19. How do we get support on the work floor?
20. How do I share my ideas?
21. How do we create sponsorship at the top?
22. How do we communicate ideas to the right people?
23. How do we convince stakeholders they benefit?
24. It does not work in our company.
25. How do we get consensus on a solution?

WITH INNOVATION

MARKET INSIGHTS

PROCESS & TOOLS

TEAM

26. Our customers don't know what they want.
27. We struggle to get inside the head of the customer.
28. How do we uncover true customer needs?

29. Our innovation process is not organized.
30. There are too many ideas.
31. We do not stick to the idea and take the easy way.
32. How do we decide what is a good idea?
33. We don't know when to stop ideas.
34. We don't know how to make ideas happen.
35. How do we select of the right technology?
36. How do we translate user studies into technology?

37. How do we guide innovation in line with strategy?
38. We do not have the right people.
39. We do not have the talents needed.
40. Teams cannot think beyond our current successes.

Source: massive response on a post in 20 LinkedIn Groups.

Harvard Business
Review:

It's tough change and within the

when markets your people company don't.

You Can't Innovate Alone

My first innovation job was marketing dried soups for Honig, the leading Dutch brand and market leader in the Netherlands. We sold around 50 million consumer packets in the Netherlands per year. Not a bad figure, considering the country's population is only 16 million. Honig had a market share of more than 60 percent. There was just one problem; the dried soups market had stopped growing.

As 'the new kid on the block', I was invited to provide fresh input into their marketing and innovation strategy. Together with the senior managers we did field research on how consumers used our soups, researched consumer trends, investigated what our competitors, Unilever and Knorr, were working on and looked into new technologies. We concluded our current market would not be able to generate growth. Therefore we knew we had to innovate and do something unique. This was in the late 1980s, the era when microwave ovens were becoming commonplace in European households. A lot of other food producers were already innovating in fresh, frozen or chilled microwavable meals that took seconds to cook. We believed we had to be part of this new market.

In addition to being involved in market strategy, senior management also had me take on a hands-on innovation assignment of my own. My challenge was to increase the long term sales of, *Honig Vermicelli Bouillon Soup*, the instant soup mix in our assortment with the lowest sales, some 750,000 packets sold annually. It was an old-fashioned clear soup with lots of vermicelli noodles. Studying the world of soup broths, one thing struck me. Broth cubes were a success as were clear broth beverages. However, our broth soup with vermicelli noodles was not. Why not just leave out the noodles? And, that's exactly what we did. We re-launched the soup as the first clear broth soup without noodles. And what happened? Sales doubled within 1 year to 1.5 million packets and margins rose by 50 percent as we saved on the costs of producing and packaging the vermicelli.

In the meantime, we discussed our chilled soups market strategy with our colleagues at R&D, logistics and production on a mid-management level. None of them liked our intention to introduce ready-made chilled soups to Honig's line of products. In their opinion we didn't have the recipe expertise and lacked the R&D capabilities. We also did not have a clue about refrigeration logistics needed to get the product into the supermarkets. We considered our colleagues foolish for once again resisting change. We then decided to take our plans to the top and got ourselves a two-hour time slot in the board room of Honig. We presented the board with all the consumer food trends and growth figures of ready-made microwave products worldwide. We even provided taste tests of competitive fresh chilled microwave products. The board was truly enthusiastic, up until we discussed the business case. This strategy was only going to be profitable after five years in the most optimistic scenario. Both costs and risks were huge as we had to build a new processing and packaging factory for chilled soups. I will never forget the words the CEO said to me at the end of the strategic innovation discussion: "Gijs, without any risk you doubled profits of our 45th selling flavor of dried soup. Innovate the 44th soup flavor and

you'll realize more profits in the coming five to ten years than with an entire line of chilled soups …" And that's just what Honig did. It continued to be a very successful market leader in dried soups. Fifteen years later H.J. Heinz bought the brand.

The wise lesson I learned as a young marketer is that in an organization you cannot innovate alone. You need an awful lot of colleagues and bosses to share your vision before a big change can truly take place. Therefore you have to give them a chance to discover for themselves what different paths are possible, what

can be developed and what is realistic. If you want to be an effective innovator, then don't make my mistake. Remember the soup lesson: you can't innovate alone. Look for the right moment to involve top management. And let them participate in your innovation expedition.

10 REASONS TO INNOVATE

CUSTOMER

JURISDICTION

TECHNOLOGY

CHANGING NEEDS AND WANTS

NEW REGULATIONS

NEW CUSTOMER GROUPS

NEW TECHNOLOGIES

MARKET LIBERALIZATION

NEW DISTRIBUTION CHANNELS

GROWING TURNOVER AND PROFITS

CREATING INNOVATIVE MINDSET

NEW BUSINESS MODELS

BOOSTING ENTREPRENEURSHIP

SHAREHOLDERS

COMPETITION

PERSONNEL

10 *Problems at the Start of Innovation*

Many things can go wrong during the process of creating new products, services or business models. Let me give you ten examples from my own experience. You may recognize this as an array of all too familiar scenarios. If so, rest assured, you are not alone.

1. We´re not sure what we want. Ideation of new products and services happens ad hoc, usually at a time when a problem arises or the turnover decreases suddenly or when a competitor enters the market unexpectedly. The first question is: "What now?" Then the creed becomes: "We'll get Smith to create a list." From this moment it becomes clear that any current strategic business plans no longer provide much direction for innovation. Ultimately, the lack of clear directives leads to random thought processes and frustration. Frustration because the management, further down in the innovation process, decided to concentrate on something else than what you were focusing on before.

2. We keep coming up with the same thing again and again. When there is a need to get ideas for new products and services, a group of people are summoned together for a brainstorming session. This session usually takes place during a long and tiring day. It's usually the same mix of colleagues, (known as the creative team) who are brought together, but nothing ever seems to materialize. That's because when you attempt to brainstorm with close colleagues you run the risk of becoming easily irritated by the predictability that comes from knowing one another´s personalities and preferences too well. Everyone automatically makes a dash for the same goal. The result is that nothing new appears and everyone leaves the meeting disappointed. At these moments they share a feeling of failure, which no one is able to prevent.

3. Sticking to conventions. Organizations have ample customer information at their disposal, do regular research into the market and are in daily contact with customers, but this process has become routine. Companies pay more attention to their current market share and what the competitor is doing right now. Prod-ucts start to look alike because everyone is copying each other´s market successes. This in turn leads to common conventions in the market while the organization loses sight of what the customer really wants. As a result of this tunnel vision, management develops a 'blind spot'. This makes room for a new competitor to appear unexpectedly with another kind of product, which just might meet some changing demand in the market.

4. The dominator. Not everyone will be given a fair chance at a brainstorming session unless there is an expert facilitator. In most cases the dominating forces are either the extroverts or the most senior managers. This makes things extremely difficult and tactically awkward for the manager in charge of leading the session. Especially when his or her manager has to have the final say in the brainstorming session and the rest of the group is silenced.

5. The negative spiral. There are brainstorming sessions where everyone has his say. After all, this is the reason for the brainstorming session, isn't it? Indeed, when you carefully listen, you can start building on the product ideas put forth by others. However, the risk involved is that ideas will be judged with immediate criticism. Remarks such as: 'That doesn´t work for us', 'We´ve tried it before', 'We´ll never get permission to do that', or 'there´s no way that can be done'. In reality, these negative statements squash real creativity. A spiral of negativity kills any chance of creativity because everyone is silenced within a short period of time.

6. We´ve got hundreds of post-its. Now what do we do? You generated ideas non-stop at a brainstorming session and covered a wall with post-its. Then, somewhere the process stalls. Where to next? Some good ideas might be among all those post-its; but the question is: how do we make heads or tails of this clutter and choose a concept? I have to admit, in the days when I was still a manager, I didn't have the answer to this either. I thought I had to find the answer on my own. I would thank all the participants for their input and take all the post-its back to my office, where they would just stare at me for weeks, until I finally threw them into the wastepaper basket. There are many places where a brainstorming session can derail.

7. Ideas remain vague. When everything in a brainstorming session goes well and creativity is stimulated, new ideas are often expressed in beautiful, poetic sounding jargon. Be aware! This might be a self inflicted pitfall. Vague statements such as: 'We are going to make an app whereby we can reach adolescents with trendy virtual mobile marketing', or 'It is going to be a very original product as its authenticity

will appeal to the primitive man inside us'. Ideas at this stage can either represent everything or represent nothing at all and still have a long way to go.

8. The management pre-kill. Ideas are screened at the beginning of the innovation pipeline. This is the often done by senior management to reset priorities during the process. Even though the goal is to innovate in a serious way, the most far-reaching ideas are the first ones removed from the equation; either because management is unable to relate or considers the idea be too far-fetched. The responsible innovators are then left wondering: "Wasn't the intention supposed to be serious innovation?"

9. The development team re-designs. It is great when the final decision is made to develop a new product idea. Subsequently the concept will transfer from the product inventors to the product developers – usually a multi-disciplinary team under the control of a project leader. It seems odd, but usually at this stage most of the life gets sucked out of an idea. The members of the development team have their own opinions as to the direction the product should take and they start dissecting the original idea. It can be helpful. It could be necessary to improve the idea during the development process. What often happens though is that the original product

idea starts to look more like something we already had, as it was easier to produce that way. The risk is that you're throwing out the baby with the bathwater.

10. Line management resistance. During development, the product idea regularly has to be 'sold' to the line management. Should the product reach the finish line of the innovation process, line management will be the ones producing the product and putting it on the market. While you might be expecting applause for your innovation, you end up getting constant comments and questions. Questions you may not have all the answers to. It is only natural to wonder if these comments and questions are meant as genuine practical arguments or whether you have fallen victim to corporate politics or the dreaded ´not my idea´ syndrome. Resistance from line management can also be attributed to their regular workloads. When they don´t have the time to develop their own ideas, they will not be prepared to spend time on the ideas of others that are imposed on them. Hence, it can happen that a good new product idea is kept in the freezer for years due to a lack of internal support. It is possible that you recognize the above-mentioned situations. Do not despair; you are not alone. And from studying the journeys of great explorers, I can provide solutions.

5 Ideation Dilemmas Solved

Ideation of new products, services or business models is difficult. Research published in the *Economist* shows that nearly 60 percent of companies have difficulty generating sufficient innovative ideas.[1] If you want to avoid problems at the start of innovation, you first have to ask yourself a series of questions. There are at least five choices you have to consider:

1. **When: now or later?**
2. **Who: external experts or internal team?**
3. **What: revolutionary or evolutionary ideas?**
4. **Which criteria to use?**
5. **How: the creative or structured way?**

1. When: now or later? It's a myth that companies are continuously innovating. Of course companies all have a R&D or innovation department working on new concepts. And a lot of big corporations even have a stage-gate innovation funnel full of new initiatives, which they monitor on a permanent basis. But if you define innovation strictly as "something really different" a lot of so-called innovations are in reality additions to or variations on existing product lines and brands. Often the innovation board of the organization will only approve genuine innovation once far less risky concepts have stopped generating growth.

The completion of the innovation process, from conception to introduction, spans an average of 18 to 36 months. So, it is extremely important to anticipate and react in time to be a market leader. Leaks in the roof are easy to spot when it's raining, but it is better to have the repairs done beforehand. The ideation process can only succeed if the company is financially and mentally sound enough to do this. If the board of directors and co-workers are under a lot of pressure you should think twice before starting an ideation project. It is best to wait until the dust has settled and the forecast is clear.

2. Who: external specialists or internal team? Would a small group of external specialists create better ideas than a group of internal managers and co-workers? They might. However, what's the use of brilliant ideas if there's no support within the organization?

Every idea might be rejected because of the 'not invented here' sentiment. You promote positive energy and cooperation within your organization by letting those colleagues, who will play a role in the development and introduction process, participate in the ideation of their own innovations. This is very helpful in the innovation delivery phase. It helps a lot if several people share in fostering an idea. For this reason I support a team approach. What's more motivating than watching your ideas take seed and flourish?

3. What: revolutionary or evolutionary ideas? Which innovation type should be your goal for a new product, service or business model: revolutionary or evolutionary? Evolutionary ideas are typically the "superior" concepts: the better supermarket, the better car rental service or the better street sweeping machine. They are often upscale innovations, which offer more at a higher price. Revolutionary concepts are truly different. Consider the origin of the *TomTom* product line. Existing manufacturers of built-in navigation systems had focused their strategy on the automobile industry and dealers. From the start, *TomTom* focused on consumer needs. Their route planners were considered consumer electronics and *TomTom* thereby needed to set completely different criteria for the product, such as: portable, easy to use and affordable. The first *TomToms* were half the price of their competitors. *TomTom* revolutionized the market in 2004 and opened a whole new consumer market for route planners.

The type of innovation you should focus on depends on the characteristics of your market, your company and your ambitions. If you are a market leader in an existing market, with low potential for growth, you should dare to go for new-to-the-market revolutionary innovations in other market segments. However, if you're a relatively small newcomer in an enormous growth market, then I can imagine you would first want to conquer the existing market with new evolutionary concepts.

4. Which criteria to use? Often an ideation project gets started when a senior director says: "We have to come up with something new." And then he or she leaves the rest up to you. And how many times has it happened that when you presented your innovative business ideas they were all rejected? It's very hard to meet fuzzy expectations. Success starts first by clearly establishing the criteria that new concepts must meet. Discuss with your Board questions like:

How much turnover must the new concept realize in year three after introduction?
What's the minimum profit margin?
Should the new concept be new to the company, new to the market or new to the world?
Should our aim be a specific target group or market?
To what extent should the new product concept be the talk of the town?
To what extent should the new product concept fit the current brand values?
Are we obliged to make the new product concept ourselves (with our own manufacturing facilities) or can we look for partners?

Making expectations explicit before you start will provide you focus.

5. How: the creative or structured way? Creativity plays a major role ideating new innovative concepts. A lot of people think you can only be creative if you don't have any constraints to consider; enabling you to really think outside the box. I agree you can't discover new oceans unless you lose sight of the existing shore. However, it's not just crazy ideas that your organization is looking for. It's looking for ideas that meet the criteria we just discussed. Therefore you need to follow a process that will lead you to concrete business cases that are attractive and viable within your organization. Creativity alone will not get you there. You will also need customer understanding, business sense and technical expertise. That's why a structured ideation approach can be a helpful tool in determining: What to do? In which order? When? With whom? And how? That's why I developed the FORTH innovation method.

1. The Economist Intelligence Unit (2008). "The Innovators: How Successful Companies Drive Business Transformation", p 10.

Albert Einstein, physicist:

If you always always did, get what you

do what you
you will always
always got.

FULL STEAM AHEAD

1 Innovation focus workshop
2 Core team intro meeting
Ideation team
Forth planning
1
3 Kick-off workshop
Innovation assignment
Departure document
6-10 innovation opportunities
Potential target groups

BAY OF DOUBTS: DO WE REALLY NEED TO INNOVATE?
FAILED BRAINSTORM WRECKS
CUSTOMERS DON'T LIKE IT' BAY

BUSY BUSY BUSY ESCAPE HARBOUR
BUSINESS AS USUAL SAND BANKS
WE INNOVATE ANYWAY
MY BOSS WON'T LET ME ISLAND

OBSERVE & LEARN

4 Explore preparation workshop
Best innovation opportunities
8 4 Observe & Learn workshops
2
5 Exploring trends & technology
An open mind
6 Discovering customer frictions
7 Exploring innovation opportunities
Best customer frictions

CUSTOMERS ARE SCARY CLIFFS
OUR OWN BLIND SPOTS
THE CALM BEFORE THE STORM PASSAGE
IT'S NOW OR NEVER CURRENT
POST-IT STORM

TEST IDEAS

12 2nd concept improvement workshop
4
3-5 improved tested concepts
11 Concept testing

ME-TOO TRIANGLE
'NOT INVENTED HERE' CLIFFS
NO SUPPORT CLIFFS
WARM CREATIVE GULF STREAM

RAISE IDEAS

500-750 ideas
30-40 idea directions
9 New product brainstorm
3
12 improved concepts
12 concepts
10 1st concept improvement workshop

'AM I CREATIVE?' TIDE

HOMECOMING

3-5 mini new business cases
15 Concept transfer workshop
THE BEST COACHES ARE IN THE SANDS WATCH TOWER
5
14 Final presentation
13 4 mini new business case workshops
An innovative mindset
An effective ideation process

WE CAN DO IT' MIST

FORTH
INNOVATION METHOD

LEGEND
☼ INNOVATION CLIMATE
➡ STAGES
✳ ACTIVITIES
◉ DELIVERABLES

➡ FULL STEAM AHEAD .... 5 WEEKS
➡ OBSERVE AND LEARN .... 6 WEEKS
➡ RAISE IDEAS .... 2 WEEKS
➡ TEST IDEAS .... 3 WEEKS
➡ HOMECOMING .... 4 WEEKS

THE FORTH INNOVATION METHOD

Inspired by great explorers like Columbus, Magellan, Amundsen, Hillary and Armstrong the method I developed for ideating new concepts is a 20-week expedition in which we'll realize a concrete innovation mission and bring back three to five mini new business cases for innovative concepts. Going on an expedition means you'll stop racing down your 'business-as-usual-highways' where you see the same familiar things. You'll explore and visit new sources of inspiration that draw you out of your comfort zone and enlarge your world, preparing you to create new and wonderful concepts.

The urgency of Magellan, the meticulous planning of Amundsen, the focus of the Apollo program, the courage of Columbus and the teamwork of Hillary's conquest of Mount Everest are all part of it. The method has the characteristics of a real expedition, mixed with best practices of creative and business thinking and is -fittingly- designed as a map. Having a map to consult is tangible proof of preparedness. And a large-scale map on the wall with a planned route inspires the crew with all the confidence it needs. Enough even to sail off the map like Columbus did.....

The innovation method for the ideation phase is called FORTH - an acronym found in the first letter of each of the 5 steps: *F*ull Steam Ahead, *O*bserve & Learn, *R*aise Ideas, *T*est Ideas and *H*omecoming. This method was developed in practice and is used successfully in both B2B and B2C markets and by non-profit organizations.

The FORTH method starts with drafting a concrete innovation assignment. And fifteen weeks after the kick-off, the team presents three to five mini new business cases to the senior management. It's a practical method for the creation of a new concept from idea to mini new business case.

During the first step, Full Steam Ahead, you immediately choose the innovation focus. Here you choose your destination and draft an innovation assignment. During the second step, Observe & Learn, you discover and understand what the potential target group considers to be important and what they struggle with the most. Furthermore, this step also includes an important condition necessary for generating new ideas: a period of incubation - in other words time to allow ideas to hatch. You will be consciously tackling your assignment as well as subconsciously. Sometimes an idea will enter your mind when you least expect it: in the shower, while on holiday or out jogging. The acquisition of insight into customers' needs and the opportunities available, as well as 'outside-in' thinking lays down the groundwork necessary for step three: an effective, creative process in Raise ideas. Ideas are generated, evaluated and developed into concrete concepts. The last two steps of the expedition concern testing the appeal of the concepts and building support. During step 4, Test Ideas, the newly developed concepts are tested among the potential target group. In the fifth and final step, Homecoming, the most promising concepts are worked out as mini new business cases and presented to the members of senior management, who have been anxiously waiting in anticipation for the unveiling of the expedition's homecoming.

I have learned from experience that the FORTH method takes about 20 weeks. For the team members, it takes approximately 15 weeks following the kick-off workshop.

In the next section the main features of the five steps are discussed.

STEP 1: FULL STEAM AHEAD

When you go on an expedition, you increase your chances of success by being well prepared; much like Roald Amundsen did to be first at the South Pole. At the start you make four very important decisions:

1. What is the innovation assignment?
2. Who is the internal client?
3. Who would make the ideal ideation team?
4. Which innovation opportunities will be explored?

The Innovation Focus Workshop

First, you have to determine a concrete goal. Together with those who are going to evaluate the new concepts at the end of the ideation phase you will draft an innovation assignment, containing which criteria the concept has to meet and the planning of the expedition.

The Ideation Team

You will have to put the team together and decide on the size of the group and who to invite. From experience I find that 14 people is the absolute maximum, made up of 12 internal FORTH team members with the option of bringing in two external members for the brainstorming process. 'Core' team members go through the whole process very intensively. This requires, from the kick-off, a period of about 20 days over fifteen weeks. Extended team members experience the process less intensively- just the highlights. They could be, for example, the internal client, other members of the board or managers. For them, the FORTH method requires approximately seven days. The number of core team members is dependent on how many business cases you want to deliver. A good mini new business case requires the efforts of two core team members. Mostly the core team varies between 6-10 people generating 3-5 mini new business cases. Make sure that you choose a well-balanced internal team.

The FORTH Kick-Off Workshop

The FORTH kick-off workshop is a full-day program striving to achieve three things. First, it is important to break through existing ways and to allow the participants to get acquainted in a creative way. Secondly, the team has to get acquainted with the content of the innovation assignment. Third, we jointly generate innovation opportunities with great potential in realizing the innovation assignment. What potential customer groups will we visit? And which experts, organizations or companies will be a potential source of inspiration?

Going Full Steam Ahead takes about five weeks. An enthusiastic, multidisciplinary team will then be ready to go on an innovation expedition.

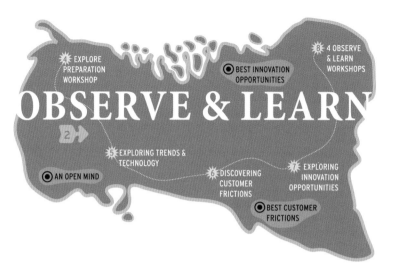

STEP 2: OBSERVE & LEARN

The essence of step two is to start viewing things differently, to detach yourself from your own existing thought patterns, and to gain new and fresh impressions. The core team members each explore an innovation opportunity and start to discover customer frictions. They report their findings to each other and to the extended team members in Observe and Learn workshops. During this step the team learns in three ways:

1. Which trends and technology can we take advantage of?
2. Who are the customers and what frictions are they struggling with?
3. Which innovation opportunities offer promising perspectives?

Exploring Trends and Technology

You start exploring different trends and technology that play a role within the parameters, theme or markets of the innovation assignment. In this way the team gets an overall view of what is going on. Promising trends and technology can then be traced and given a role during the new product brainstorming session in the next step.

Meeting Customers

The fundamental question is: who are the customers and what are they concerned with? Meeting with customers in person and finding out the frictions of the customer with the help of focus groups belong to the most effective techniques when wanting to create new product ideas. This technique has been confirmed by a previously mentioned recent American study concerning ideation techniques.[1]

It is of the utmost importance to know how the product is being used or which role it plays in a specific production process. Current behavior of customers and the visible difficulties experienced, create an excellent source of inspiration. In this step, all team members will pay a visit to customers to get their own personal impression of their concerns and experiences.

Visits to Sources of Inspiration

All innovation opportunities are explored by the core team members. They contact the selected sources of inspiration and visit them individually in order to explore the direction. In this way they search for the best practices in other companies and for valuable experiences from various other people or companies.

The Observe & Learn Workshops

In four Observe & Learn workshops, core team members share their experiences. During the last Observe and Learn workshop all team members choose the most appealing innovation opportunities and customer frictions. These will be in the spotlight during the brainstorming session in the next step together with the promising trends and technologies.

Observe & Learn lasts six weeks. The ideation team has discovered relevant customer frictions and promising innovation opportunities.

STEP 3. RAISE IDEAS

This step is the pièce de résistance. It consists of a two-day new product brainstorming session and a concept improvement workshop. It is the creative peak of the expedition.

The New Product Brainstorming Session
New concepts are developed with a structured creative process in nine steps during a two-day high-energy brainstorming session. By the end of the idea divergence process, some 500 to 750 ideas will have been generated. The 12 best concepts are selected to be worked out.

The 1st Concept Improvement Workshop
In a dedicated workshop, the core team members improve all concepts produced during the new product brainstorming session before they are tested on potential customers.

Raise Ideas takes just two weeks. The ideation team has developed twelve new concepts for innovative products, services or business models.

STEP 4: TEST IDEAS

How appealing are the new concepts and how many really stand out? Let's reflect on them with customers.

Concept Testing
The appeal of the new concepts is tested directly among the target group on a limited scale to get insight into what was or wasn't liked. It's done in personal in-depth interviews, focus groups or online research. The core team members follow the testing live so they can find new inspiration and make immediate improvements.

The 2nd Concept Improvement Workshop
Based on customer feedback in a brainstorming session, team members find ways to further improve the new concepts. At the end of this workshop, three to five concepts are chosen to be worked out in detail for the presentation of the mini new business cases.

Test Ideas takes three weeks. The ideation team tests twelve new concepts of which three to five are chosen to be developed into mini new business cases.

3-5 MINI NEW BUSINESS CASES

THE BEST COACHES ARE IN THE SANDS WATCH TOWER

CONCEPT TRANSFER WORKSHOP

HOMECOMING

5

FINAL PRESENTATION

4 MINI NEW BUSINESS CASE WORKSHOPS

AN INNOVATIVE MINDSET

AN EFFECTIVE IDEATION PROCESS

STEP 5: HOMECOMING

In the final step, the FORTH expedition returns home with three to five attractive new product or service concepts and enough support to fill the innovation pipeline. Homecoming is the climatic step of the 20-week journey.

The Mini New Business Case Workshops

In core team duos, the best concepts are worked out as mini new business cases in four full-day workshops. The advantage of drafting mini new business cases is that it makes every team member aware that not just creative aspects, but also commercial, professional and financial aspects contribute to the decision to adopt the new concepts for further development in the innovation process. In addition, it strengthens the concepts, as they are based on strategic, commercial, technical and financial indicators.

The Final Presentation

It is very important to get those who have not been working closely with the FORTH innovation method, enthusiastic about the con-

cepts. An 'outside the box' presentation of the FORTH expedition, in the form of a guided tour in their own 'innovation room', is usually a good way to get them involved. Next, it is important to present the mini new business cases to the senior managers who make the official decision whether or not to develop a product.

The Concept Transfer Workshop

The ideation phase ends with the adoption of the new concepts into the development process. After the decision has been made to develop the new concepts, a concept transfer workshop organizes the transfer of responsibility from the ideation team to the development team and is also responsible for securing the essence of the concept.

Homecoming takes about four weeks. The expedition ends there with three to five attractive new product or service concepts with internal support for development.

The good news is that all FORTH expeditions returned home safe and successful. Furthermore, participants in the past have all described it as an unforgettable experience. Many of whom felt that the journey itself was just as rewarding as the expedition reaching its destination successfully.

GO TO THE WEBSITE AND DOWNLOAD ALL THE CHECKLISTS OF THE FORTH INNOVATION METHOD
www.forth-innovation.com

1. Robert G. Cooper, Scott Edgett (March 2008). Ideation for Product Innovation: What are the Best Methods? *PDMA Visions*.

THE 66-POINT INNOVATION CHECKLIST

The fuzzy front end is the nickname for the start of innovation or innovation phase. Why? Because getting innovative ideas is a vague process. It's considered hard to do. That's exactly why I like to unfuzzy it. Connect creativity and business reality in five steps: Full Steam Ahead, Observe and Learn, Raise Ideas, Test Ideas and Homecoming. Here is a practical 66-point innovation checklist to help you.

FULL STEAM AHEAD

1. "If you always do what you always did, you will always get what you always got." [Albert Einstein].
2. Create momentum for your innovation project. There must be urgency otherwise innovation is considered as playtime and nobody will be prepared to go outside the box.
3. Manage the expectations of your bosses and the line management before you start your innovation project(s).
4. It is essential to start your innovation journey with a clear and concrete innovation assignment to give focus.
5. Be concrete about the market/target group for which the innovations must be developed.
6. Define which criteria the new concepts must meet. This forms the guidelines throughout the process.
7. Use a team approach to improve innovation results and increase internal support for the innovative outcome.
8. "They always say time changes things, but you actually have to change them yourself." [Andy Wharhol].
9. Invite people for whom the innovation assignment is personally relevant.
10. Invite people for both content and decision-making.
11. Be sure to invite people who think outside the box.
12. Also include a few outsiders.
13. Get a good mix of men and women, young and old, and so on.
14. Let top management participate in the innovation team.
15. Identify potential target groups for innovation.
16. "The reasonable man adapts himself to the world; the unreasonable persists in trying to adapt the world to himself. Therefore all progress depends on the unreasonable man." [G. Bernard Shaw].

OBSERVE & LEARN

OBSERVE AND LEARN

17. "Man cannot discover new oceans unless you have the courage to lose sight of the shore." [André Gide].
18. It is essential to get fresh insights before you start creating ideas.
19. Ask questions.
20. Use web searching and crowd sourcing to open up the minds of the innovation team: what do we learn from this?
21. Postpone your judgement.
22. Ask the most important question again and again: why?
23. What are the trends among potential target groups? Why?
24. What are emerging relevant new technologies? Why?
25. Visit customers, observe their behaviour and ask yourself the question: why?
26. Visit companies in other sectors that serve as a source of inspiration to discover innovation opportunities. Ask yourself: what do I learn from this?
27. Look for problems: start discovering relevant customer frictions to solve.

RAISE IDEAS

RAISE IDEAS

28. "The best way to have a good idea is to have lots of ideas." [Linus Pauling].
29. Look for a special environment for your innovation workshops (special place, special theme, special music, special food et cetera).
30. Create an emotionally safe environment where you can be yourself.
31. Focus 100%: do not ever allow ringing and flashing iPhones and Blackberrys.
32. Never, I really mean never, brainstorm at the office.
33. Take at least two days for an effective brainstorming session for concrete new concepts.
34. Plan and prepare an effective combination of idea generating techniques.
35. Spend twice as much time on the convergence process as on the divergence process.
36. Make sure the innovation workshops are enjoyable. Fun promotes good results.
37. Monitor all participants and simultaneously involve them in the innovation process.
38. Time box. Work with strict deadlines. They help you to get people thinking outside the box. And to make choices.
39. Be open to ideas or suggestions from your innovation team to adapt the process.

40. Allow people to choose which innovation opportunity, idea, concept board or mini new business case they want to work on.
41. Appoint an (internal) expert facilitator, who oversees everything while remaining in the background.
42. As facilitator give the opposite energy to the group. If the group is too active: be calm. If the group is too calm: be more energetic.
43. Visualize the results.
44. Keep up the momentum; otherwise it becomes long-winded and the team will get bored.

TEST IDEAS

45. "The audience liked it, so I kept it in. I would try a line and leave it in too if it got a laugh. If it didn't, I'd take it out and put in another." [Groucho Marx].
46. Check the strength of the newly created concepts right away at the front end.
47. Great ideas are the ones appealing to customers.
48. Use the voice of the customer internally to get support.
49. Use online tools to check ideas if speed is important.
50. Successful innovations will solve relevant problems of customers.

51. Check if the innovation fits the brand.
52. Would you really use this concept yourself?
53. Use customer feedback to improve the concepts.

HOMECOMING

HOMECOMING

54. Return with mini new business cases instead of post-its or mood boards.
55. "If you have enough information to make a business case, you're too late." [Bill Gates].
56. Come back with innovative concepts that fit the in-the-box reality of your organization, otherwise nothing will happen.
57. A good concept stands out in the market.
58. "The best ideas lose their owners and take on lives of their own." [Nolan Bushnell].
59. Attractive innovations realize extra turnover.

60. Ideas get approved when they have adequate profit potential.
61. Be sure innovations fit management's personal goals.
62. You only get support when innovation is (somehow) considered feasible.
63. Winning new concepts give potential customers a concrete reason to switch.
64. Make use of the specific expertise of others from within the organization as much as you can in an early phase in the innovation process.
65. Substantiate, in a businesslike and convincing manner, to what degree and for what reason the new concept can meet the criteria.
66. "Ideas are useless unless used." [Theordore Levitt].

GO FOR IT! FOLLOW YOUR PASSION AND MAKE YOUR INNOVATION DREAMS COME TRUE.

30 TIPS FOR INNOVATION SESSION FACILITATORS

1. Choose a way of working that best suits you.
2. Stay genuine and be yourself.
3. Be open to ideas from the group to adapt the program.
4. Give the opposite energy to the group.
5. Give a time box. Make sure everybody knows the time limit for an assignment.
6. Always have a clock available.
7. Always explain what you are going to do and why.
8. Have everyone use the same color post-its and pens so that it does not stand out whose idea it is and it will not influence the choices.
9. Always write clearly and concisely.
10. Check with the project leader how to divide everyone into teams.
11. Choose appropriate music to create the right atmosphere.
12. Make sure the session is enjoyable. Fun promotes good results.
13. Control the process; don't try to control each individual. Respect everyone's own space.
14. Expect the unexpected; as things don't alway go as planned.
15. During disagreements in the group, follow your own instinct, opinion and feeling.
16. Remind the group of the agreement to be respectful towards one another.
17. Give credit where appropriate; stimulate, motivate and enthuse the group publicly.
18. Let the group do the work. Not you.
19. Keep up the momentum otherwise it becomes too long-winded and the group will get bored.
20. Always stay one step ahead of the group so you can apply the next technique immediately.
21. Ask the group for help if you are not sure how to continue.
22. Always treat everyone with respect, but also tell them when you do not approve of something.
23. Pay attention to the body language of the participants.
24. Regularly check what the groups are working on so that, if necessary, you can guide them.
25. Allow people to choose which innovation opportunities, ideas or concepts they want to work on.
26. As facilitator be present, but do not overdo it.
27. Have confidence in the quality of the group and allow them to work independently.
28. Intervene only when absolutely necessary.
29. Give the project leader and the client a 'wild card' during the selection process.
30. Preparation, preparation, preparation.

III.

Full Steam
Ahead

1 INNOVATION FOCUS WORKSHOP

IDEATION TEAM

2 CORE TEAM INTRO MEETING

FORTH PLANNING

BUSY BUS

1

FULL STEAM AHEAD

3 KICK-OFF WORKSHOP

BUSIN SAND

INNOVATION ASSIGNMENT

DEPARTURE DOCUMENT

6-10 INNOVATION OPPORTUNITIES

WE I

BAY OF DOUBTS: DO WE REALLY NEED TO INNOVATE?

POTENTIAL TARGET GROUPS

MY BOSS WON T LET ME ISLAND

FAILED BRAINSTORM WRECKS

12 2ND CONCEPT IMPROVEMENT WORKSH

TEST I

STEP 1: FULL STEAM AHEAD

You never start a professional expedition unprepared. Good preparation not only increases the chances of success, but also creates priorities and the will to succeed. That is why this first step in creating new concepts is so terribly important. Full Steam Ahead illustrates how you can challenge management to start a real innovation project and how you formulate an innovation assignment during the innovation focus workshop. It also shows how you can put together the ideal ideation team with internal and external participants. All this lasts about five weeks and is the first step of the ideation phase.

Your first action is to establish the purpose and the innovation direction. In the FORTH method it is done collectively in an innovation focus workshop with both the managers concerned as well as those who will lead the FORTH project.

The agenda has four main points:
1. The innovation assignment and the criteria for evaluation.
2. The participants of the ideation team.
3. The planning of the FORTH innovation approach.
4. The total costs in time and money.

At first you have to determine a concrete aim and direction. At the same time, together with those who are going to evaluate the new concepts, you have to decide which criteria the innovations have to meet. The innovation focus workshop has only succeeded when you have collectively formulated a concrete innovation assignment and can start putting an ideation team together. In this book, you will find a practical checklist on how to draft an innovation assignment.

A very important decision to make on your innovation expedition is how your ideal team will look. The bigger the team is, the greater the diversity and the greater the chance of coming up with wild, offbeat and pioneering ideas. Through experience I have found that fourteen is an optimal team size, made up of twelve internal team members with the option of bringing in two outsiders for the brainstorming process. I usually distinguish between two roles in the team: core team members and the so-called extended team members. A core team member goes through the whole ideation process very intensively. From Kick-Off, it requires about twenty days over a fifteen-week period. Extended team members experience the process less intensely; mainly being there for the highlights. They are generally the CEO or other members of the board or senior management. Their involvement with the FORTH method requires approximately seven days in the fifteen weeks following the Kick-Off.

Make sure that you choose a well-balanced internal team. And choose the best people: always choose those who have a passion for the assignment and who possess the right qualities. A specific assignment always requires special people. However, they are usually the ones who have the least time available and therefore aren't given permission to participate. Fortunately, it is only a matter of convincing the managers. The criteria whereby potential team members could be chosen are:
Their enthusiasm and drive. Find participants who are enthusiastic about the theme and who are driven to innovate. Their unrestrained energy and passion will rub off on the group.
Their responsibility and support. You usually include participants whose work

relates to the innovation assignment fostering internal support at the same time. For example, if you include the marketing manager because it concerns the market for which he is responsible, his department will likely be more supportive.

Their knowledge and expertise. You include participants in the team based on their knowledge and expertise because this is essential for the successful execution of the innovation assignment.

Their fresh outlook and skills. You also choose outsiders to complement the internal team especially during the Raise Ideas Step. The advantage is that an outsider can bring in something extra or new.

FORTH Activity 2:
Core Team Intro Meeting

As FORTH facilitator I have found that it is a good idea to meet with the core team the evening before the official Kick-Off workshop. This is a chance to meet and share personal experiences. This should be done at the same venue where the Kick-Off workshop is being organized on the following day. It is possible that the members have had negative experiences at the start of a development process in the past, which might hamper the fresh start of the innovation project. An excellent technique on how to approach this can be found in 'The Trash Can' (see The Innovation Toolkit).

FORTH Activity 3:
Kick-Off Workshop

I usually implement a full-day program with the internal client, the project leader and the ideation team. Together we strive to achieve our four goals. First, a good personal introduction is essential. It is important to break through existing ways and to allow the participants to get acquainted in a creative way. Second, the team has to get acquainted with the content of the innovation assignment. In this respect the chairman of the board of directors plays a huge role. It is his or her task to emphasize the urgency of the innovation assignment, to explain the innovation assignment and to reach an agreement after amendments have been made. Third, it is very satisfying when you have determined, with the help of excellent pre-analysis and some creative techniques, six to ten innovation opportunities for the ideation team to explore in the next step. You can do this in practice by asking: Where are the greatest opportunities with regards to the innovation assignment? Which experts, organizations or companies will be a significant source of inspiration? Lastly, you identify with the ideation team interesting target groups you will approach in the next step Observe & Learn to dive into their theirs needs and challenges.

At the end of the five weeks you will have an enthusiastic, multidisciplinary team ready for the innovation expedition.

GO TO THE FORTH WEBSITE AND DOWNLOAD THE FOUR PRACTICAL CHECKLISTS OF THE STEP FULL STEAM AHEAD (www.forth-innovation.com/forth-steps/full-steam-ahead/)

FACTSHEET STEP 1

Duration	5 weeks
Activities	1. Innovation Focus Workshop 2. Core Team Intro Meeting 3. Kick-Off Workshop
Deliverables	1. Innovation assignment 2. Ideation team composition 3. FORTH planning 4. Departure document 5. Potential target groups 6. Six to ten innovation opportunities
Outcome	An enthusiastic, multidisciplinary team ready for the innovation expedition.
Crucial moments	1. Do we get the innovation assignment SMART? 2. Are the potential target groups clear? 3. Is there sufficient support for innovation at the top? 4. Do we have the right team? 5. Are the interrelations in the team okay? 6. Do we have insights in the challenges for the target groups? 7. Do we choose the right innovation opportunities? 8. Will the selected sources of inspiration lead us away from our daily business?
Risks	1. I would love to go FORTH and innovate. Therefore I am not so critical about meeting all preconditions to be successful. 2. The innovation assignment remains too vague because we lack the courage to choose. 3. Managers block the participation of key members of the team. 4. The sources of inspiration for our explorations in the next step are too close to our daily business.
Next step	Step 2 Observe & Learn: Explore innovation opportunities, customers' frictions, trends and technology.

Lao Tzu,
Taoist:

A journey of a
must begin with

thousand miles
a single step.

THE PERFECT INNOVATION TEAM

The Mayo Clinic's Center for Innovation, a best-practice organization which was researched in APQC's *Innovation: Putting Ideas into Action 2009* study, favors a specific combination of personalities when it builds innovation teams. The Mayo Clinic strives to include the following nine personality types when composing innovation teams:

Source: "Innovation: Putting Ideas into Action 2009 (Best Practices Report)", APQC, Houston, USA.

1. The Visionary — The force behind creating the world as it could be - and should be.
2. The Generator — The generator of the idea who gets an innovation rolling.
3. The Iterator — An idea-engineer who takes the original idea and turns it into an innovation.
4. The Customer Anthropologist — The keen observer of what customers truly hunger for.
5. The Tech Guru — The harnesser of technology to turn the innovation into reality.
6. The Producer — The champion of flow. The master of moving ideas along.
7. The Communicator — Amplifies and clarifies the idea in the minds of others outside the team.
8. The Roadblock Remover — With a hammer - or velvet gloves- knocks away organization, political, and financial roadblocks.
9. The Futurecaster — The forecaster and modeler of the economic and social value of the future of innovation.

Never Start Innovation With Just an Idea

It is a provoking title, isn't it? Never start product or service innovation with just an idea. It's true that innovation is initially about ideas. But, it's about getting the right ideas and their marketability. The global symbol for innovation is a bright, shining light bulb. Of course, it's wonderful to dream big; to have a vision and lots of ideas. However, when you are innovating within an organization, there are three reasons why you should not start with just one idea.

Blinded by an idea.

Once an idea comes to you, you'll probably fall in love with it. That's certainly a great feeling. Unfortunately, love puts blinders on. The psychological phenomenon of selective perception only lets you see the positive points of an idea and only lets you listen to people who are supportive. But down the road, when you try to get your idea off the ground, you'll run into a brick wall in 80 percent of the cases. This will wake you up. Be sure to have alternatives available to realize your business challenge.

It's very difficult to convince others.

What happens when you tell your idea to other people? Their first reaction often starts with 'Yes, but…' Others within your company will start criticizing your idea the moment it is told to them. An important reason for this is that the idea is not theirs. Furthermore companies and organizations are structured to keep a handle on the current operational processes and to give account of the results produced. Should the size and complexity of the organization increase, innovation then becomes more difficult. On your own, the innovation process may seem complex. The solution is to raise ideas together as a team so everyone can share ownership of an idea.

Fewer than two out of seven new product ideas ever reach the market.

An excellent study on new product innovation (Robert G. Cooper, 2011) showed that for every 7 new product ideas, about 4 enter development, 1 to 2 are launched and only 1 succeeds. These are very poor odds. There is only a 1 out of 5 chance that your idea will reach the market. So, what do you do when your boss, the vice president of marketing or the innovation board stops your new idea? Do you have any alternatives available to realize your business challenge?

NEVER BET ON
ONE HORSE. THAT'S
THE MAIN MESSAGE.

It's All About the Right Moment

Organizations innovate continuously. At least, that's what they say. There is a difference between what they say and what they really do. Of course there is a department continuously working on new concepts. But most of these concepts are variations, line extensions or brand extensions. Senior management will only approve real innovations when they believe all low-risk concepts have stopped generating growth.

And these are the moments you should wait for. These we-really-need-to-innovate moments often coincide with other incidents, like:

- Three continuous quarters without any growth in turnover;
- A competitor just introduced a great new product that everyone envies;
- One of your biggest clients just left;
- A new competitor entered the market with a revolutionary business model;
- You just lost three tenders in a row for a big assignment.

An effective innovator should act with the patience of a hunter:

"When it comes time to take a shot, take your time. Remember, too, that most hunters, even very experienced ones, have no business trying a shot at a running animal. All too often doing so results in a wounded deer that is never recovered. Wait for a shot that you're sure you can make."[1]

But you, the innovator, face a dilemma. You cannot wait too long. You know completion of the innovation process takes at least 18 months– from the idea to introducing it in the market. So, it is extremely important to anticipate and react in time to be a market leader. Leaks in the roof are easy to spot when it's raining, but it is better to have the repairs done beforehand. The ideation process can only succeed if the company is financially and mentally sound enough to do this. If the board of directors and co-workers are under a lot of pressure you should think twice before starting an ideation project. It is best to wait until the dust has settled and the forecast is clear.

Once you start, be sure to act swiftly. You know that a merger, strategy change or another crisis will jeopardize your innovation project. So focus and market new concepts as fast as you can.

Remember: you can only start an innovation project once for the first time!

1. Deer Hunting for Beginners, by Bruce Woods, November/December 1989 http://www.motherearth-news.com/

Andy Warhol,
artist: *They always*
things, but you
to change

say time changes
actually have
them yourself.

What's Your Innovation Assignment?

How do you start ideation in practice? Often there's a senior manager experiencing an urgent need for something new. A new competitor may have entered the market, turnover may have decreased dramatically or a big contract is lost. And something has to happen: we need to innovate. A special innovation project team is set up and starts generating ideas. However, an essential point is often missed: ideas for what? That's the question!

Do you have a clear innovation assignment yourself?

You should never start an innovation expedition unprepared. Good preparation increases the chances of success because it creates priorities, direction and the drive to succeed. That's why it is essential to start your innovation journey with a clear and concrete innovation assignment. Starting with an assignment obligates senior management to be concrete about the target market group for which the innovations must be developed and the criteria that must be met. This forms the guidelines for your ideation team when you are underway. You can formulate the innovation assignment with the help of the following six questions:

1. Why? (Why do we want to innovate?);
2. Who? (Who is the target group?);
3. Where? (For which distribution channels, countries, regions or continents?);
4. What? (Evolutionary or revolutionary: products, services or business models);
5. When? (Intended year of introduction);
6. Which? (Which criteria should the new concepts meet?).

The purpose of an innovation focus workshop is to answer the questions above together with senior management. Often your board has not yet defined the criteria the new concepts should meet. Then it helps to ask some questions. In practice you will go a long way with the following eight questions:

1. Turnover. How much turnover must the new concept realize during the first three years? Or, if new products compete with existing products, how much extra turnover must be realized?

2. Profit. What profit margin should the new concept realize?

3. New. Should the new concept be new to the company, new to the market or new to the world?

4. Appeal. How attractive and pioneering to the target group does the new product concept need to be?

5. Promotion. To what extent do we want the product concept to create buzz and hype among potential customers?

6. Positioning. To what extent should the new product concept fit the current brand positioning?

7. Production. Do we produce the new product ourselves (with our own manufacturing facilities) or can we form production partnerships?

8. Strategic fit. To what extent should the new product concept fit the business strategy of the organization?

Ideate new products and/or services for Sanoma Media to introduce successfully in the Netherlands; using the brands *Margriet* and *Libelle* in new or existing consumer markets with existing brand values for the present target group of women.

We are looking for at least three new concepts which individually will realize an annual sales potential of € 25 million with a profit margin of at least 25 percent. The new concepts should fulfill a concrete need and be attractive, distinctive and reliable to the target group. They should fit the brand values of *Margriet* and *Libelle*. They must be feasible and the business risk should be within manageable limits. To realize the new concepts and increase feasibility; partnerships or joint ventures with other companies will likely be forged. Our aim is to introduce new concepts in the market within two years.

This innovation assignment gives clear objectives and perfectly communicates the expectations of senior management to the members of the innovation team.

So, in your discussion with senior management, you will collectively formulate the criteria for the new product concepts as well as determine the ambition levels.

Below, is an actual case from an innovation assignment for Sanoma Media Netherlands. Sanoma is a leading European group in the fields of media and learning. With operations in 20 countries, its turnover was € 2.5 billion in 2011. *Libelle* and *Margriet*, two leading women's weekly magazines in the Netherlands, are both important brands for the bottom-line of Sanoma Media Netherlands. Unfortunately, the market for printed magazines has reached its peak and is declining. That's more than enough reason to look beyond the next 12 months. This is also why Sanoma wants to explore how to extend these popular brands beyond the current media market. Will it be feasible to use the *Libelle* and *Margriet* brands to launch new concepts in a completely new market? Sanoma drafted a very concrete assignment at the start of their innovation process.

THE INNOVATION ASSIGNMENT

A CONCRETE INNOVATION ASSIGNMENT

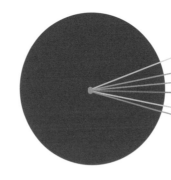

WHY DO WE NEED TO INNOVATE?

WHO IS THE TARGET GROUP?

WHAT: PRODUCTS? SERVICES? SOLUTIONS?

WHICH CRITERIA SHOULD THE NEW CONCEPTS MEET?

WHERE: COUNTRIES? REGIONS?

WHEN: YEAR OF INTRODUCTION?

THE ORIGIN OF

With special thanks to Marcel Grauls, who wanted to share this story in this book.

Bill Harley was born in Milwaukee, Wisconsin in 1880. He came from a working class family who had just arrived in the USA from Manchester, England. When Bill was fifteen, he found a job as an apprentice at a small bicycle repair shop. He loved the outdoor life and had a talent for drawing and natural history.

Two years later he found an apprenticeship as a designer draftsman at a small steel factory. It was no coincidence that his school friend Arthur Davidson was working in the foundry as a model-maker. The Davidson family had moved there from Aberdeen, Scotland twenty years before. The Davidson's were true Scots.

Harley really loved trout fishing and every weekend he and Davidson went fishing together at the numerous lakes in the Milwaukee area. Around that time, when they were still in their teens, a German who had previously worked in Paris showed up at their small factory, carrying the drawings of a Dion Gasoline engine.

First, they constructed an engine for their small fishing boat. In autumn 1900, they got the idea to put an engine on a bike.

HARLEY DAVIDSON MOTORCYCLES

The bike frame, however, was too light. In the course of 1902, Arthur got his 26-year-old brother Walter involved, who already had worked for a number of railroad workshops. By spring 1903, they had the first prototype of their motorcycle ready. Their contraption managed to reach 23mph (37 kph), but it still needed extra pedaling on the hilly back roads of Milwaukee. Naturally, that was unacceptable.

Harley designed a new and heavier motorcycle. And Davidson's father, a carpenter, built a 10 × 14-foot shed in the backyard for the boys to work in their spare time. Bill Harley thought he lacked the proper professional technical training and enrolled into a technical college that autumn. Walter Davidson gave up his job in spring 1904 to dedicate himself full time to motorcycles.

In 1904, they sold three motorcycles, all with a 50% payment in advance. They needed the buyers' money to afford supplies for the bikes. In 1905 they brought out 5 motorcycles, 49 in 1906, and 152 in 1907. At that time Arthur's oldest brother William had joined them as well.

By 1908 they had 36 employees on their pay-roll and produced 456 motorcycles. That year Walter won a spectacular motorcycle race with 84 racers at the starting line, representing 22 motorcycle companies. Walter got the record score of 1000 points and a bonus of 5 points. This was five points above the absolute maximum. The makers of 'The Silent Gray Fellow' (for its smooth running engine and gray frame) saw their business take off.

None of them lived to a very old age. William was the first to die in 1937, at the age of 66, followed by Walter in 1942 also 66. In 1943, Bill Harley died at the age 63. Then, in 1950, at the age of 69, Arthur died together with his wife in, of all things, a car accident.

Source: Marcel Grauls, *Het paard van Ferrari* (2003),
Publisher Balans en Van Halewyck, Amsterdam

IV.

Observe
& Learn

CUSTOMERS ARE SCARY CLIFFS

RBOUR

8 4 OBSERVE & LEARN WORKSHOPS

4 EXPLORE PREPARATION WORKSHOP

⊙ BEST INNOVATION OPPORTUNITIES

OBSERVE & LEARN

2⇒

5 EXPLORING TRENDS & TECHNOLOGY

⊙ AN OPEN MIND

6 DISCOVERING CUSTOMER FRICTIONS

7 EXPLORING INNOVATION OPPORTUNITIES

⊙ BEST CUSTOMER FRICTIONS

IT'S N NEVER

OUR OWN BLIND SPOTS

THE CALM BEFORE THE STORM PASSAGE

ME-TOO TRIANGLE

S

⊙ 500-750 IDEAS

⊙ 30-40 IDEA DIRECTIONS

9 NEW

STEP 2: OBSERVE & LEARN

An essential part of being innovative is to start viewing things differently. You have to detach yourself from your own existing thought patterns and habits. Albert Einstein taught us: "If you always do what you always did, you will always get what you always got." So, you need to gain new and refreshing insights. That is why this second step in creating new concepts is so extremely important. Observe & Learn illustrates how you can explore innovation opportunities, trends and technology and how you can discover customer frictions among the target groups. It also shows how you can share your findings among the ideation team in an inspiring way. The entire process takes about six weeks and is the second step of the ideation phase.

FORTH Activity 4:
Exploration Preparation Workshop

This workshop is meant to get each member of the core team geared for action. In this workshop you have the team make their final preparations with checklists and formats so they are well equipped.

FORTH Activity 5:
Exploring Trends & Technology

We start by exploring promising trends and technology relevant to the domain, theme or markets of the innovation assignment. This should increase the team's awareness of the bigger picture. The relevant trends and technology can be traced and assigned a role during the brainstorming sessions in the next step.

FORTH Activity 6:
Discovering Customer Frictions

A fundamental question is: what are the needs of potential customers? In this step you can use two very effective Voice-of-Customer techniques: meeting with the customer in person and finding out the frictions of the customer with the help of focus groups.

Customers' current behavior and the visible difficulties they experience offer an excellent source of inspiration. In this stage all team members visit customers to gather their own impressions of the customer, his or her concerns and experiences.

Focus groups are a type of qualitative research whereby groups of customers are interviewed by a facilitator. The core team members are present only to listen and observe closely. Directly following the interviews they discuss the situation of the target group and its relevant needs and frictions. One focus group is assigned to each target group.

FORTH Activity 7:
Exploring Innovation Opportunities

During the Kick-Off activities, innovation opportunities have been generated and adopted by the core team members. In this step core team members will explore their innovation opportunities. They contact selected groups outside the business as sources of inspiration and visit each one individually. They investigate best practices and search for valuable ideas from other people or companies. Their findings are shared for evaluation in the Observe and Learn workshops.

FORTH Activity 8:
Observe & Learn Workshops

The members of the core team go on a six-week hike where they gather new impressions and share them with one another and the extended team members in four Observe and Learn workshops. During the last Observe and Learn workshop they choose the most promising innovation opportunities and customer frictions. These will then be put under the spotlight alongside the promising trends and technologies during the brainstorming session in the next step.

By the end of the second step the ideation team is really inspired, having discovered promising and relevant customer frictions and innovation opportunities.

GO TO THE FORTH WEBSITE AND DOWNLOAD THE FOUR PRACTICAL CHECKLISTS OF THE STEP OBSERVE & LEARN (www.forth-innovation.com/forth-steps/observe-and-learn/)

FACTSHEET STEP 2

Duration	6 weeks

Activities	1. Explore Preparation Workshop 2. Exploring Trends & Technology 3. Discovering Customer Frictions 4. Exploring Innovation Opportunities 5. 4 Observe & Learn Workshops

Deliverables	1. Best customer frictions 2. Best innovation opportunities 3. Open-mindedness towards all team members

Outcome	Highly inspired ideation team has discovered promising and relevant customer frictions, trends, technology and innovation opportunities.

Crucial moments	1. Following the Kick Off workshop, core team members soon arrange their visits to outside sources of inspiration. 2. Core team members speaking up during the interviews. 3. Core team members share their findings in a way that is inspiring. 4. Judgment is deferred during Observe & Learn workshops. 5. Extended team members give the floor to the core team members and listen well to what they have to report. 6. Core team members learn to think from the perspective of customer frictions. 7. Discovery of relevant customer frictions. 8. Choosing the best customer frictions and innovation opportunities.

Risks	1. Core team members are too timid about taking the initiative to make appointments on their own. 2. Dominant extended team members lack good listening skills and don't defer judgment. 3. The focus group consists of the wrong mix of people. 4. The exploration spends too much time staying inside-the-box.

Next step	Raise Ideas: Ideating and improving twelve concepts from more than 500-750 ideas.

The Operational Excellence Excuse

Operational excellence is "a philosophy of the workplace where problem-solving, teamwork, and leadership results in the ongoing improvement in an organization. The process involves focusing on customer needs, keeping the employees positive and empowered, and continually improving the current activities in the workplace."[1]

In practice companies implementing this philosophy tend to focus on only doing things better and cheaper. In an economic crisis, companies misrepresent operational excellence for cost cutting purposes. Cost cutting is essential to keep companies profitable, but only for the short term. In the long run your business cannot indefinitely survive by improving its product at a lower cost. In times of crisis, operational excellence is used as an excuse to focus on costs, cutting into innovation budgets as one of the first.

This operational excellence does not reverse trends though. Better and cheaper newspapers couldn't stop digital news. Better and cheaper postal services couldn't stop email. Better and cheaper medical doctors couldn't stop nurse practitioners. Better and cheaper recruiting couldn't stop overseas outsourcing. Better and cheaper stores couldn't stop e-commerce.

New technology, new regulations, new entrants and new business models disrupt markets. Only doing things better won't help you. Besides upgrading you should be looking for groundbreaking ways to innovate your company. In fact, did you know that operational excellence can also be used to encourage genuine innovative ideas which provide value to customers and the organization?

But there are no old roads to new destinations. Where should you look? Be inspired by the famous words of the historical Apple campaign of 1997: Think Different.

Here's to the crazy ones. The misfits. The rebels. The troublemakers. The round pegs in the square holes. The ones who see things differently. They're not fond of rules. And they have no respect for the status quo. You can quote them, disagree with them, glorify or vilify them. About the only thing you can't do is ignore them.

Because they change things. They push the human race forward. While some may see them as the crazy ones, we see genius. Because the people who are crazy enough to think they can change the world, are the ones who do.

Don't just do things better; that will only kill you in the end. Think different at the right moment. Hear the misfits, the rebels and the troublemakers. Think change.

1. www.businessdictionary.com

THINKING LIKE A DESIGNER

Thinking like a designer can transform the way you approach the world when imagining and creating new solutions for the future. It's about being aware of the world around you, believing that you play a role in shaping that world, and taking action toward a more desirable future. Thinking like a designer requires five characteristics.

"TO INVENT A FUTURE THAT DOESN'T EXIST, YOU REALLY HAVE TO UNDERSTAND WHAT PEOPLE ARE DOING TODAY AND COMPLETELY RE-IMAGINE IT."

1. Empathy. The empathic thinker can imagine the world from multiple perspectives – those of colleagues, clients, end users, and customers. By taking a "people first" approach, design thinkers can imagine solutions that are inherently desirable and meet explicit or latent needs. Great design thinkers notice things that others do not and use their insights to inspire innovation.

2. Integrative thinking. The integrative thinker not only relies on analytical processes but also exhibits the ability to see all of the salient – and sometimes contradictory – aspects of a confounding problem and creates novel solutions that go beyond and dramatically improve on existing alternatives.

3. Optimism. The optimistic thinker assumes that no matter how challenging the constraints of a given problem, at least one potential solution is better than the existing alternatives.

4. Experimentalism. The experimental thinker believes significant innovations don't come from incremental tweaks. Design thinkers pose questions and explore constraints in creative ways that proceed in entirely new directions.

5. Collaboration. The increasing complexity of products, services, and experiences has replaced the myth of the lone creative genius with the reality of the enthusiastic interdisciplinary collaborator. The best design thinkers don't simply work alongside other disciplines; many of them have significant experience in more than one.

Sources: Design Thinking Toolkit Ideo/Riverdale Country School, 'How Thinking Like a Designer Can Inspire Innovation' by Nadia Goodman www.entrepreneur.com, 'Design Thinking' by 'Tim Brown' Harvard Business Review June 2008.

Anonymous: *The fish is who will*

the last one discover water.

10 ELEMENTS OF AN

1

• People who can manage relationships with customers and partners: If you're going to open up your organization to ideas from the outside, then you need *"agile and people who have the soft skills of emotional intelligence."*

2

• A willingness to accept that not *all* of the smart people work at your company: At the same time, to be successful at open innovation, your organization's culture must not just accept this idea intellectually, but also have a willingness to seek out these outside ideas.

3

• An understanding that failures are learning opportunities; and a willingness to reward those efforts and that way of learning. *"Failure is a way of life for companies that pursue innovation seriously, and a leader's response has a huge effect on company culture and, therefore, on future projects."* Celebrate failure and learn from it!

4

• A willingness to help employees build the knowledge and understanding of how an idea or technology becomes a profitable business.

5

• Dismiss the Not-Invented-Here syndrome: *"If we make the best use of internal and external ideas, we will win. We don't need to own everything ourselves and keep it under tight wraps. We should profit from others' use of our innovation process, and we should buy others' intellectual property whenever it advances our own business model."*

OPEN INNOVATION CULTURE

Source: Stefan Lindegaard, *The Open Innovation Revolution: Essentials, Roadblocks and Leadership Skills*, Wiley, 2010. www.innovationmanagement. se "10 essential elements of an open innovation culture", June 9, 2010.

6

• A willingness to strive for balance between internal and external R&D. *"External R&D can create significant value; internal R&D is needed to claim some portion of that value."*

7

• Willingness to be a risk taker rather than being risk averse.

8

• Accepting that open innovation does raise intellectual property issues.

9

• Understanding that open innovation requires open communication. *"Work around confidentiality and intellectual property issues to create an environment based on trust."*

10

• Not needing to always be first. *"Building a better business model is better than getting to market first."*

How to Get Rid of Old Ideas?

Innovation is all about getting new ideas for simple solutions to solve relevant customer problems or needs. When there is a sudden need for innovation the first thing people do is organize a brainstorming session. But usually this approach doesn't lead to anything innovative. That's why brainstorming has such negative connotations in a lot of companies. Because, when you brainstorm unprepared with the same group of colleagues, hardly anything new will appear. And you'd think not getting any new ideas would be the problem. But you'd be wrong. The problem is getting rid of the old ideas first!

I love this quote by the American businessman Dee Hock:

"The problem is never how to get new, innovative thoughts into your mind, but how to get old ones out. Every mind is a building filled with archaic furniture. Clean out a corner of your mind and creativity will instantly fill it."

Once you've got the old ideas out of your mind, new ones come automatically! That's why it is essential that you first change your thought patterns to get rid of the old ideas before you can create new ones. Key to breaking old thought patterns is acknowledging that they are outdated and keep you from the progress you really desire. You won't convince yourself of this by staying behind your desk. You have to go out there to challenge your old insights. There are many ways to replace old ideas with new insights:

1. Explore trends
By exploring trends yourself, you will realize the world is changing rapidly. Trends offer inspiration for new insights. So study new concepts or business models based on new trends. And see that there are all kinds of emerging market offerings. Refer to the checklist with 18 international top trend sites as a starter.

2. Explore technology
Technological developments are a wonderful source of inspiration. You will find technological resources in your own country as well, such as universities of technology, research centers linked to non-profit government agencies or large tech companies such as Google, Philips, Siemens or Vodafone. And, get into contact with market leaders such as Samsung, 3M, IBM or Cap Gemini to explore their new technology. Soon, you'll find out that the way you have been doing things is fast becoming obsolete.

3. Explore Opportunities
Generate potential innovation opportunities and seek inspiring sources for those opportunities. Go out and meet with inspiring people. One thing will lead to another. Your exploration journey will automatically take you off the familiar highways your mind usually follows.

4. Explore Customer Frictions
Meeting customers in person and discovering their frictions are the most effective sources of inspiration when it comes to getting rid of old ideas. A customer friction is a relevant need, impulse or wish from a specific target group, which is currently left unsatisfied. Often, these are issues people struggle with daily in their personal and professional lives. You just have to get out there; meet and talk with them, always asking the most important question: why?! Remember: "The man who asks a question is a fool for a minute, the man who does not ask is a fool for life." [Confucius].

You
need fresh,
new insights
to get fresh,
new ideas.

7 TIPS
FOR AN INNOVATIVE
WEB SEARCH

What is the fastest way you can find ideas, inspiration and innovation opportunities on the web? Stop searching and start using these seven tips to directly find the most unique and relevant sites during your discovery.

1. Proper off line preparation

You shouldn't blindly start a Google search. It's better to start by meticulously writing down your conditions for a query:

- What are the five to seven essential terms in your query?
- Search sites in languages other than English and translate the key words in three other languages (via Google Translate).
- Imagine the ideal page answering your queries. What do these ideal answers look like? Use this exact same wording as a search query.

2. Use all of Google's possibilities.

Hundreds of extra search options are hidden behind Google's 'minimal' homepage.

- Always use 'Google advanced' and select, when needed, language, country, file format, date, et cetera.
- Always use at least three query terms and use parenthesis when these words have to be searched together.
- There are a number of specific channels on Google. Explore your query also in Google images, scholar, video, news, blogs, directory, et cetera.

3. Solo brainstorming

By now, you have settled into your query. Take time to gain some perspective. After all, you're looking for something still unknown to you. So, you can't realistically expect to find an answer via Google. Therefore, it is best to imagine possible cases that you hope to find on the net. Come up with a list around your query of over fifty new product or service ideas. The weirder, the better. Consequently, do a search on the net for these imaginary products. You'll automatically end up on sites you wouldn't usually find.

4. There's more out there than Google

It's time to leave Google, as Google only offers us a small fraction of the Internet. An ideal starting point is http://www.browsys.com/finder/. You'll find numerous search engines that are well categorized (general, images, video, news, social, files, reference, academic). You'll also notice right away that you can query in very diverse formats. It is also highly recommended to search through social media such as Twitter, LinkedIn Groups, et cetera.

5. Search in different languages

Install the Google Toolbar, it will immediately translate foreign language sites to English. The translations are far from perfect, but good enough to give you the general idea. For example, if you need to find information on innovations related to food or gadgets, just query some Japanese sites. First imagine which countries have a lot of expertise in the domain you're researching, then go and explore them.

6. Deep web search

A lot of information is not directly accessible via Google. A lot of diverse sources (large databases, libraries and archives) have to be queried directly. That's why you need to scout (via Google) your main sources and then, one-by-one, research these sources with your query. You can also perform a deep search by smart multiplication. Imagine you've found one well-hidden super source around your query. Then use Google to find out who else talks about this site. Most likely you'll discover another valuable source. Consequently, combine both sources in Google and you will most likely discover a third and a fourth. Combine all four and you will end up on a site belonging to someone who already collected the information related to your original query.

7. Find ideas from other sectors

Three tips to combine ideas from other worlds with your query:
- RSS Feeds: Don't just subscribe to sites around your domain, but also subscribe to at least ten other sectors and areas of interest each month.
- Search for a sector that is somewhat related, where the level of innovation is higher than in your sector. Consequently check if these innovations can be translated to your query. Take this query for example: how can I avoid lines at the cash register? Then try a search for innovations concerning traffic congestion on the road.
- Make a list of the most innovative companies that are currently out there. Then imagine how they would innovate in your domain. Some examples: How would Nike innovate public transportation? How would Virgin design a new cell phone? How would Cirque du Soleil innovate hotels and restaurants?

Source: Marc Heleven, web search professional, www.7ideas.be.

18 TOP INTERNATIONAL TREND SITES

Springwise
Springwise scans the globe for the most promising business ventures, ideas and concepts that are ready for regional or international adaptation, expansion, partnering, investments or cooperation.
www.springwise.com

Trendwatching
One of the world's leading trend firms, trendwatching.com scans the globe for emerging consumer trends, insights and innovations.
www.trendwatching.com

Trendhunter
Trend Hunter is the world's largest, most popular collection of cutting edge ideas, crowdsourced by 85,462 Trend Hunters.
www.trendhunter.com

NOTCOT
NOTCOT Inc is a growing network of design sites currently including NOTCOT.com and innovative community contributed sites NOTCOT.org + NotCouture.com + Liqurious.com. NOTCOT is a visual filtration of ideas + aesthetics + amusements.
www.notcot.org

More Inspiration
MoreInspiration lets you discover innovative products and technologies from all possible domains.
www.moreinspiration.com

PSFK
Over 1,000,000 readers from the design, digital, marketing, media and technology industries come to PSFK each month to read and share emerging ideas.
www.psfk.com

Trends@alltop
The purpose of Alltop is to help you answer the question, 'What's happening?' in 'all the topics' that interest you. You may wonder how Alltop is different from a search engine. A search engine is good for answering questions like, 'How many people live in China?' However, it has a much harder time answering the question, 'What's happening in China?' That's the kind of question that Alltop answers.
trends.alltop.com

CoolBusinessIdeas
CoolBusinessIdeas.com is a blog about brand new promising business ideas around the world. Follow them in the hunt for the latest business concepts!
www.coolbusinessideas.com

Trendcentral
Powered by the research, insights and global trendsetter network of The Intelligence Group, trendcentral® focuses on what's new and what's next in the realms of lifestyle, fashion, entertainment and technology. Over the years, trendcentral has forecast the arrival of cultural phenomena well before they entered the mainstream, ranging from branded designer jeans and vampire films to videoblogging and Twitter.
www.trendcentral.com

World Future

Our mission is to enable thinkers, political personalities, scientists and lay-people to share an informed, serious dialogue on what the future will be like.
www.wfs.org

David Report

David Report is an influential blog and online magazine that since 2006 writes about trends in the intersection of design, culture and business. Our readers share our interest and curiosity in everything from art, architecture, culture, design and fashion to food, innovation, music, sustainability and travel.
www.davidreport.com

TED

TED is a nonprofit devoted to Ideas Worth Spreading. It started out (in 1984) as a conference bringing together people from three worlds: Technology, Entertainment, Design.
www.ted.com

JWT Intelligence

We focus on identifying changes in the global zeitgeist so as to convert shifts into compelling opportunities for brands. We have done this on behalf of multinational clients across several categories including pharmaceuticals, cosmetics, food, home and personal care.
www.jwtintelligence.com

Copenhagen Institute for Futures Studies

The objective of the Copenhagen Institute for Futures Studies is to strengthen the basis for decision-making in public and private organizations by creating awareness of the future and highlighting its importance to the present.
www.cifs.dk/en/

Lidewij Edelkoort

From her creation of innovative trend books and audiovisuals since the 1980s to lifestyle analysis and research conducted for the world's leading brands today, Lidewij has pioneered trend forecasting as a profession.
www.edelkoort.com

TrendOriginal

TrendOriginal is the personal consumer trends collections of Dr. Taly Weiss, CEO and head researcher for TrendsSpotting. com Market Research and founder of TrendoScope-The trend spotting lab.
www.trendoriginal.com

Cool Hunting

Cool Hunting is synonymous with seeking inspiration. Our global team of editors and contributors sift through innovations in design, technology, art and culture to create our award-winning publication, consisting of daily updates and weekly mini-documentaries.
www.coolhunting.com

Mashable

Mashable is the largest independent news source dedicated to covering digital culture, social media and technology. Mashable's 20 million monthly unique visitors and 4 million social media followers have become one of the most engaged online news communities.
www.mashable.com

With special thanks to, web search professional, Marc Heleven,
www.7ideas.be

Innovators Look for Problems

One of the main reasons innovation is difficult, is because your potential users need to change their behavior. They will have to find, buy and use your innovation. And why should they? That's the question! You will have to give them a strong reason why! This applies both to consumers and B2B markets.

Ask yourself the question: when was the last time I changed my own behavior? We are all stuck in our habits; doing things in fixed patterns. We as innovators do this as well. For years, we go on reading the same journals, buying the same cars and staying with the same insurance company. The only reason for us to change is if a new, simple and attractive solution comes along that is relevant to our lives. I guess I can make it as simple as that.

Simply put, effective innovation is all about matching relevant problems with simple solutions. You can approach it two different ways. One way is to create the ideas and solutions first and later try to match these to target groups with problems relevant to your solutions. Or you can do it the other way by first identifying the relevant problems of the target groups and then creating ideas and solutions to solve those problems.

I'd like to inspire you with a list of ten practical problems and innovative new products or services solving them.

Problem	Solution
Consultant: I need new assignments. How do I expand my business network in an efficient way?	*LinkedIn*
Music lovers: I love listening to music for free, but I hate to be a pirate downloading it illegally.	*Spotify*
Consumer cleaning: I'm sick and tired of a poorly performing vacuum cleaner.	*Dyson Cyclone vacuum cleaner*
Consumer: Is this bed clean and free of bugs I can hardly see?	*The Bed Bug Detective*
Snowboarder: I'd like to go downhill fast, but I am afraid of nasty accidents.	*The Katal Landing Pad*
Consumer painting: If there is one thing that really annoys me, it's cleaning used brushes and rollers.	*Dulux PaintPod*
Green consumer: I hate wasting water and money flushing the toilet.	*Brondell Perfect Flush*
3rd world countries: We lack clean drinking water due to flooding.	*Filtrix Filterpen*
Full-time mother: Now that the kids are older, I'd like to re-enter the workforce, but who is looking for someone like me?	*Work4Women*
Green consumer: I love to celebrate Christmas with a real tree, but don't like destroying nature.	*Lease a living Christmas tree*

But how should you go about finding relevant problems among your target groups? Here are five ways to help you in practice:

- Visit customers at their homes or companies and get acquainted with them.
- Have your customers demonstrate how they use your product and observe how it's used in practice.
- Invite customers to focus groups and listen to their issues.
- Ask customers which products in your domain are their favorites and why.
- Crowdsource customer problems by asking customers to post their input on issues, suggestions, improvements or ideas on relevant places on the web.

*Get out there
and just do it.*

Robert Frost, poet: *Two roads in a wood and*

*diverged
I took the one less
traveled by.*

HOW TO FIND

Meeting (potential) customers in person and talking to customers in focus groups belong to the most effective techniques for creating new product ideas. A previously mentioned recent American study concerning ideation techniques confirms this.[1] It is of the utmost importance to know how existing products or services in the domain of your innovation mission are being used or which role they play in a specific production process in B2B markets.

The proper preparation will help you to find customer frictions. There are three important questions to answer:

1. Who are the relevant customers?
2. How do we discover what their concerns are?
3. How do we describe the customer friction?

1. Identifying relevant customer groups

In both B2C and B2B markets, you need to ask yourself the question: Who is involved in the decision making process in the relevant domain for this product/service category? Identify different roles, like:

1. The Initiator - who starts the purchasing process?
2. The Influencer - who tries to convince others they need the product?
3. The Decider - who makes the final decision?
4. The Buyer - who is going to pay the bill?
5. The User - who ends up using your product or service?

Another way to identify customers is based on their usage:

1. Non-users.
2. Light-users.
3. Average-users.
4. Heavy-users.
4. Ex-users.

Select the customer groups based on roles or usage most relevant to you. Identify matching consumers or professional customers, who you can contact and visit personally or invite to join a focus group discussion.

CUSTOMER FRICTIONS?

2. Discovering what their concerns are

Stepping into the lives of consumers or professional customers is THE way to discover issues people are concerned with. Person-to-person interviews work quite well as they are conducive to building mutual trust and make the participants more inclined to tell you what bothers them in the product/service domain you'd like to discuss with them. Focus groups are also a good option if the subject is not too sensitive. The script used to discover customer frictions is quite similar for personal interviews and focus groups:

- Tell me about yourself.
- Tell me about the relevancy for you of products/services in this domain. Why?
- Tell me about your buying experience. Why?
- Tell me about the usage of these products/services. Why?
- On buying/using: What are you struggling with? Which problems do you encounter? Why?
- What would be your ultimate dream in this domain? Why?

As you noticed, the key question is: WHY?

3. Describing the customer's friction

In recognizing struggles, problems of customers, carefully listen to what they say. A lot of times a real friction will start with "BUT..." A very handy format describing customer frictions contains three elements.
A. Situation: Describes the personal characteristics and situation of the customer.
B. Need: Describes the needs of the customer.
C. Friction: Describes the problem or struggle of the customer.

Let me give you a concrete example of a friction in Northern Europe among women ages 30-50 with children:
A. Situation: I am a housewife and mother of two children.
B. Need: I would love to be more than the mother of..... or the wife of..... and would like to go back to work again.
C. Friction: But I am afraid that I won't be able to combine a part-time job with my responsibilities at home. Besides that, temp agencies don't like to employ mothers.

Tip: The art of describing a good customer friction is to write it down in plain customer language and keep it as simple as possible.

1. Robert G. Cooper, Scott Edgett (March 2008). "Ideation for Product Innovation: What are the Best Methods?" PDMA Visions.

11 BRILLIANT INVENTIONS MADE BY MISTAKE[1]

EAST INDIES

AMERICA

Some of the most popular products were happy accidents. Serendepity: the accident of finding something good or useful while not specifically searching for it.[2]

1. Columbus. Columbus's personal goal was to seek wealth by establishing a new trade route and reach the East Indies by sailing westward. On October 12, 1492 he sighted land. He called the inhabitants Indians being sure that he had reached the Indies. But he discovered the Americas.

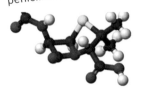

2. Penicillin. Alexander Fleming left a pile of dirty petri dishes stacked up. In one of them mold had blocked the bacteria and penicillin was identified.

1. Inspired by Tom Donnelly,' 9 Brilliant Inventions Made by Mistake', Inc.com August 15th, 2012.
2. Wikipedia.org.

3. The Slinky. In 1943, Richard James developed fragile springs to keep equipment steady on ships. When he took it home, his wife saw the potential for a new toy: the Slinky.

4. Post-it-Notes. Spencer Silver tried to develop a superstrong adhesive in 1968. He invented the opposite. Colleague Art Fry saw a new way to mark pages in his hymnbook.

5. Wheaties. In 1922 a clumsy dietitian spilled a wheat bran mixture on a hot stove. It turned into flakes that tasted much better than the original..

9. Corn Flakes. In 1894 the Kellogg brothers were called away after cooking some wheat. When they came back, the wheat had become stale. They decided to force it through rollers. The wheat berries were flattened into flakes and then baked. After experimenting with other grains, Corn Flakes were born.

7. Plastics. Hyatt accidentally spilled a bottle of collodion, to discover it formed a flexible-yet-strong material. His brother Isaiah coined the term celluloid to describe the first commercially successful plastic.

8. Saccharine. In 1879 chemist Constantin Fahlberg rushed off for a meal with his hands all still covered in laboratory goo. He broke a piece of bread, put it to his lips, and noticed it tasted unusually sweet.

10. Pacemaker. In 1956, Greatbatch was working on building a heart rhythm recording device. He reached into a box and pulled out a resistor of the wrong size and plugged it into the circuit. When he installed it, he recognized the rhythmic lub-dub sound of the human heart.

Color Mauve. In 1856, chemist William Perkin was working on a creating an artificial version of the malaria drug quinine. Instead, his experiments produced a dark oily sludge: inventing synthetic dye.

11. Coke. Pharmacist John Pemberton was trying to make a cure for headaches in 1886. He mixed together a bunch of ingredients. It took eight years of being sold in a drug store before the drink was popular enough to be sold in bottles.

THE ORIGIN OF

With special thanks to Marcel Grauls, who wanted to share this story in this book.

Saturu Iwata, president of Nintendo, believes in the "blue ocean" business theory. For a company to succeed, its target should be a blue ocean: a place without competitors. Companies who enter a bloody red ocean, full of aggressive rivals, will have a substantially lower chance of success. With the traditional games becoming more and more realistic, the products were only appealing to young men ages 18-35. What about targeting families, women, small children and seniors? That's why the Brain Age games line that was recently introduced targeted the older generation. That's why the Wii series introduced: Wii Fit, Wii Music, Wii Sport. That's why a Wii doesn't have a joystick or two-handed controller, but comes with a wireless Wiimote: a bar with moving sensors which displays the player's motions on the screen.

The driving force behind all of this is Shigeru Miyamoto, the creator of 70 percent of all the Nintendo games. He has been dubbed 'the Spielberg' or 'the Walt Disney' of video games. Miyamoto was the first one to introduce a storyline and characters to video games. The stories are always based on his own experiences. The Wii-Fit is as well. "Around my forties I started gaining weight and started swimming to lose weight. After a while this really worked, but then I started to neglect my weight again and gained

it all back. My wife suggested buying a good scale, one that could measure the fat percentage as well as the weight. This really got me interested in measuring my weight. I hung up a graph in my bathroom tracking my weight and fat. Wii Fit originally was named 'Health Pack' and was nothing more than a new kind of digital scale to connect to your original Wii. In Miyamoto's brain it was only a small step to the Wii Fit balance board, which customers are buying by the millions each year.

Shigeru Miyamoto was born on November 16, 1952 in Sonobe, a small city fifty kilometers north east of Kyoto. He grew up surrounded by nature. He fished in rivers, ran through rice fields and rolled down hills. In those days, his parents, both teachers, didn't have a TV at home. In the evenings, Shigeru's parents would take him to the Noh theater, Kabuki dance drama or Bunraku puppet theater. On several occasions they traveled by train to Kyoto to shop or go to the cinema. As a young boy, Shigeru watched Disney's Peter Pan and Snow White. He loved reading, drawing and painting. He handcrafted intricate puppets that he used in his own puppet theater. One day, while out exploring, he discovered a cave in a nearby forest. After some hesitation, he got the courage to enter the cave armed with a flashlight he had made himself. Inside he found another entrance that led deeper into the cave and he continued to proceed with his heart pounding. He never forgot the excitement he felt at that moment. In all

Wii AND SUPER MARIO

the games that he would later develop, he tried to create the same sense of thrill from those childhood experiences.

Later on, the Miyamoto family moved to Kyoto. Shigeru dreamed about being an artist, puppeteer or a painter. He always had paper and a pencil with him and made drawings of nature or comics: especially the popular manga comics. In 1970, he started his study as industrial designer at the University of Kanazawa. He was not really a hardworking student and it took him five years to graduate instead of three. He drew, listened to music, taught himself to play guitar and studied country music. He performed together with banjo accompaniment in coffee shops and at parties in Kyoto. After he graduated, he was clueless about which profession to choose. He father contacted an old acquaintance of his, Hiroshi Yamauchi, the boss of Nintendo. "We need engineers, not artists." Yamauchi had said. Nevertheless, Shigeru was invited to pay him a visit. Ninetendo historian Shepp described Miyamato's appearance like this: a 24-year-old, with wild hair and a smile like the cat who just ate the canary. Yamauchi asked Shigeru to come back with some ideas for toys. He came up with coat racks with pegs shaped like a bird or an elephant's head; all with rounded edges so children couldn't hurt themselves. He was then given a job at Planning. This was in 1977. One of Miyamoto's early assignments was not ideating games, but designing cabinets for video arcade games. >>

THE ORIGIN OF

Since 1980, Nintendo had been trying to conquer the American market with its arcade games. But it was failure after failure. Finally, Yamauchi asked Miyamoto if he could ideate a new game. As a student Miyamoto played many video games: the usual shooting games in video arcades. You had to shoot enemy planes, which came right at you. He found them uninspiring. He had often wondered why these games did not contain a storyline like in books or movies. Why couldn't games be interpreted as his favorite stories, fairy tales and legends like King Kong? And that was the moment he came up with a storyline about a sweet King Kong, who belonged to a crazy carpenter who treated him badly. The game consists of an elaborate chase through a construction site with different levels and various obstacles along the way. The gorilla kidnapped the carpenter's girlfriend and ran up to the seventh storey of a house under construction. Being chased by the carpenter, the gorilla would then throw barrels of cement at the carpenter. Players could help the carpenter to jump over the barrels. And that's how the carpenter got his original name: Jumpman. Reaching the top storey, the chase continued over the steel beams. Now forcing the carpenter to escape the flames and falling beams. Once the entire structure has collapsed, the carpenter and his girlfriend are finally re-united. The carpenter needed to be a bit weird. Miyamoto started with a big nose and two big eyes. The engineers taught Miyamoto that the body should be clearly visible, so he chose striking clothes and

big arms. As it was difficult to make the hair move in conjunction with every movement, Miyamoto put a red cap on the carpenter's head. Miyamoto even wrote the music for the game with the help of an electric keyboard.

As Yamauchi wanted to enter the American market, the game had to have an English name. But Miyamoto hardly understood English. In Japanese he came up with the name "Stubborn Gorilla". In the English dictionary under "stubborn" he found the word "donkey" and from "King Kong" he took the word "Kong". It wasn't until much later that Nintendo realized the name Donkey Kong didn't make sense in English. The Nintendo team who had to market the new game in the United States was astonished after having had so many failures in the past. They changed the name of the carpenter from "Jumpman" to "Mario", because the character resembled Mario Segali the landlord of the branch building rented by Nintendo. Despite the team's protests Yamauchi stuck to the name Donkey Kong. And in 1981 Donkey Kong became Nintendo's first smash hit in American arcades.

Nintendo's top designer Gunpei Yokoi, employed at Nintendo since 1965, needed some help with ideating new games for his Games & Watch. He asked Yamauchi if he could ask Miyamoto for help, who immediately developed an adaptation of Donkey Kong. Another top designer at Nintendo, Uemada was look-

ing for new games for the game console Famicon NES. Again Miyamoto was invited to the big boss' office. Miyamoto again re-invented the carpenter character. After someone had told Miyamato that Mario really looked more like a plumber than a carpenter, he transformed Mario into a plumber. It was one of Miyamoto's wishes to let two people play a game together. So, he ideated a brother for Mario, called Luigi, who was all dressed in green. This storyline for the Famicon was developed into the game 'Super Mario Bros' and was released in 1984. It became one of the best-loved video games ever.
Shigeru Miyamoto still contributes to the success of Nintendo. He currently manages the Nintendo Entertainment Analysis and Development branch which employs 400 people and handles many of Nintendo's top-selling titles. In his team he is known for a special habit that he has, a phenomenon, which the Japanese call 'chabudai gaeshi'. This means literally 'upending the tea table'. Figuratively this stands for Miyamoto saying, "Stop! Start all over from zero."

In March 2005, he was one of the first people to receive a star on San Francisco's 'Walk of Game'. The game series of Donkey Kong, Mario and Zelda alone, have sold more than 350 million worldwide. He has been chosen repeatedly by *Time* Magazine as one of the most influential people of our contemporary culture.

Source: Marcel Grauls, *Gewoon Geniaal*, Publisher Van Halewyck, October 2009.

V.

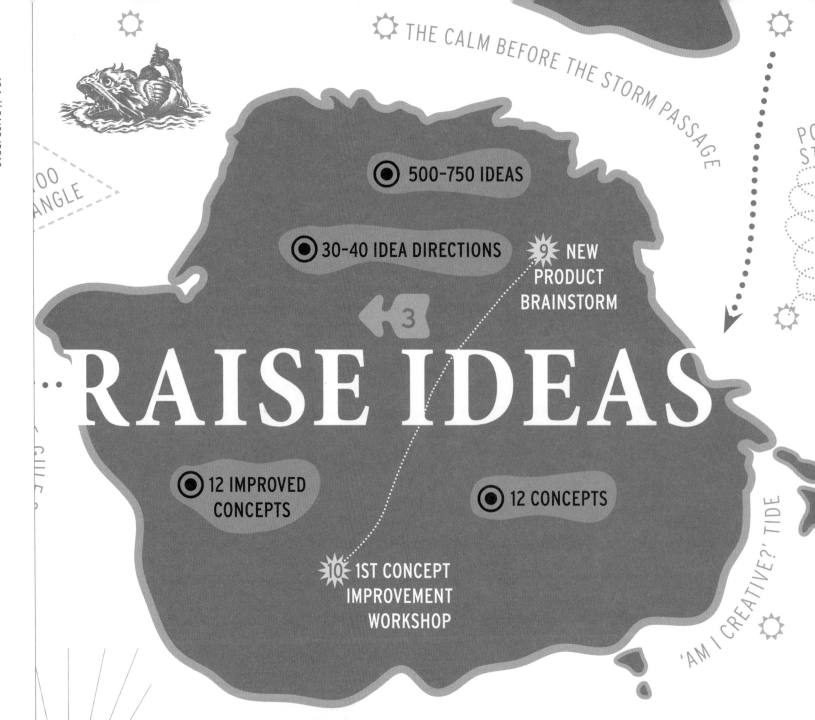

THE CALM BEFORE THE STORM PASSAGE

500-750 IDEAS

30-40 IDEA DIRECTIONS

9 NEW PRODUCT BRAINSTORM

3

RAISE IDEAS

12 IMPROVED CONCEPTS

12 CONCEPTS

10 1ST CONCEPT IMPROVEMENT WORKSHOP

'AM I CREATIVE?' TIDE

STEP 3: RAISE IDEAS

This step is the pièce de résistance. It consists of a two-day new product brainstorming session and a concept improvement workshop. The brainstorming session is where the new ideas are actually prepared and developed into a concept. These concepts for new products, services or business models are further developed during the concept improvement workshop. The innovation opportunities, the discovered customer frictions, the involvement of outsiders and an effective creative process are all part of the third step. It is the creative peak of the expedition. Raise Ideas takes just two weeks and is the third step of the ideation phase.

FORTH Activity 9:
New Product Brainstorming
New concepts are developed with a structured creative process in nine steps during a two-day high-energy brainstorming session. After a creative warming-up exercise of the mind, idea-generating gets into full swing. Participants finally have the opportunity, after six weeks, to unleash their ideas in a spontaneous 'brain dump'. The outsiders will bring new ideas and will inspire the innovation team members and vice versa. In the divergence phase, which follows, the participants are led outside the box with the help of different brainstorming techniques. This will generate many new and original ideas: on average 500 to 750 ideas. Subsequently, the convergence phase starts. All new ideas are condensed into 30 to 40 different directions. The participants choose the twelve idea directions with the most potential and develop these into idea mind maps. On the second day, small groups develop the idea mind maps into concrete new business concepts. At the end of three one-hour sessions, twelve concepts will be ready. The participants now present their concepts during a short presentation where input from the group improves the concepts. Each participant then evaluates the concepts individually. Their evaluation is based on the criteria established in the innovation assignment at the beginning of the expedition. During the completion of the process all developed concepts are discussed in order of attractiveness and it is not uncommon that, at some point, a spontaneous feeling of WOW develops.

FORTH Activity 10:
1st Concept Improvement Workshop
At the brainstorming session the concepts were evaluated. In addition to their strong points, points for improvements were also identified. In a dedicated workshop, the core team members improve all concepts before they are tested on potential customers.

At the end of Raise Ideas, the ideation team has developed twelve new concepts for innovative products, services or business models.

GO TO THE FORTH WEBSITE AND DOWNLOAD THE FOUR PRACTICAL CHECKLISTS OF THE STEP RAISE IDEAS
(www.forth-innovation.com/forth-steps/raise-ideas/)

FACTSHEET STEP 3

Duration	2 weeks
Activities	9. New Product Brainstorming Session
	10. 1st Concept Improvement Workshop
Deliverables	1. 500-750 ideas
	2. 30 to 40 different idea directions
	3. 12 concepts
	4. 12 improved concepts
Outcome	Twelve new concepts for innovative products, services or business models; all ready for concept testing.
Crucial moments	1. The right brainstorming venue and an informal atmosphere.
	2. Outsiders joining the brainstorming session integrate well in the group.
	3. Defer judgment during the idea-generating process.
	4. A lot of new ideas are generated before lunchtime.
	5. Ideas get outside the box.
	6. Finding the rights descriptions for the idea directions.
	7. Choosing the top 12 idea directions.
	8. The 'right click' in the concept-making groups.
	9. Team members show ownership of their concepts.
	10. First responses on the overall ranking of concepts.

Risks

1. The brainstorming venue sucks.
2. Crucial team members are late.
3. Smartphones and iPads interrupt the process.
4. Team members can't defer their judgment.
5. Team members can't think outside the box.
6. Discussions formulating the different idea directions.
7. Dominance of top management.
8. Uncertainty between day one and day two if the ideas are the right ones.
9. Endless discussions in the concept-making groups.
10. Wrong interpretation of the criteria evaluating the ideas.
11. Disappointment that their concept has been negatively evaluated.

Next step

Test Ideas: Testing and improving twelve concepts with customers and making a choice which three to five concepts to work out as mini new business cases.

Linus Pauling, chemist: *The best* *a good idea*

*way to have
is to have lots
of ideas.*

THINK LIKE STEVE JOBS

THE ESSENCE OF
JOBS' UNIQUE GENIUS:
UNDERSTANDING THAT ABSENCE DEFINES
PRESENCE; THAT THE ONLY PATH TO THE GREAT
NEW THINGS OF THE FUTURE WAS THE MERCILESS
ELIMINATION OF THE GOOD OLD THINGS
OF THE PAST.

Shut Up in a Brainstorm for Better Results

The spiritual father of the brainstorming technique is the American Alex Osborn. He is also one of the founders (and the 'O') of advertising agency BBDO, still renowned worldwide. In 1948 he published a book called *Your Creative Power*. In the chapter "How to Organize a Squad to Create Ideas" he describes when a group works together, the members should engage in a "brainstorm," that is; "using the brain to storm a creative problem – and doing so in commando fashion, with each stormer attacking the same objective." Two essential rules are: 1. 'Defer your judgment' and 2. 'Go for quantity'. The underlying assumption of brainstorming is that people are scared of saying something wrong. In a period where employees still were scared to speak up, brainstorming was experienced as revolutionary.

Since the fifties a lot of people have challenged the effectiveness of brainstorms. Keith Sawyer, a psychologist at Washington University, once summed up the science to conclude: "Decades of research have consistently shown that brainstorming groups think of far fewer ideas than the same number of people who work alone and later pool their ideas." Recent research of Bernard Nijstad and Wolfgang Stroebe confirmed that brainstorming in a group has two major shortcomings.

1. Individuals often produce fewer ideas and ideas of lower quality in group settings as compared when they work alone.
2. When people have to wait for others to complete their turn before presenting their idea, ideas are often lost.

Nijstad elaborated to say that being part of a group only gives you the illusion of group productivity. His findings show that group members are more satisfied with their performance than individuals, despite having generated fewer ideas.

The group setting makes you feel more productive. This feeling is attributed to the group experiencing fewer instances in which someone is unable to generate ideas.

Why then do I recommend a two-day new product brainstorming session with fourteen participants? Luckily, brainstorming has evolved since the fifties. Back then, it was common practice that all participants could spontaneously shout out their ideas. This led to chaotic situations whereby the individual

thought process was constantly interrupted. Furthermore, in large brainstorming groups most participants had to wait too long before they could unleash their ideas, which caused some ideas to vanish before anyone even had a chance to hear them.

Being aware of the pitfalls of generating fewer ideas and lower quality ideas, I fine-tuned the brainstorming method. The brainstorming approach on a FORTH innovation expedition is done differently. Team members first get the

opportunity to start generating new ideas in complete silence. They each write their ideas on separate post-it notes. Afterwards, everybody quickly reads their ideas out loud to the group. This has a very stimulating effect on the participants as they are encouraged to continue listening and to elaborate on their own ideas. How the participants are positioned in the room also has a stimulating effect as they are seated in a horseshoe formation (without tables) and can see each other clearly. This way, the idea of one participant is a source of inspiration for the other. Brainstorming this way for four rounds using different techniques usually leads to 500 – 750 ideas on the idea wall. The experience of sharing, selecting and drafting concrete concepts from the best ideas has a great impact on group dynamics. At the end, the whole group feels ownership of the concepts. That is essential. New concepts need a lot of parents to survive a corporate culture.

Sources:
1. Wikipedia 2. The New Yorker, "GROUPTHINK: the brainstorming myth, by Jonah Lehrer, 30 January 2012. 3. Bernard Nijstad, How the Group Affects the Mind: Effects of Communication in Idea Generating Groups, 2000. 4. The illusion of Group Productivity: a Reduction of Failures Explanation, Bernard Nijstad, Wolfgang Stroebe, Hein Lodewijkx, European Journal of Social Psychology, Volume 36, Issue 1, pages 31–48, January/February 2006.

IDEA KILLERS

Our customers won't like that!

It already exists!

Yes, but...

It's not possible...

NO!

We need to do more research...

That's not logical...

Let's be realistic...

It's too expensive!

We don't have time...

I'm not creative...

The management won't agree...

THERE'S NO BUDGET...

IT IS NOT SUITABLE FOR OUR CLIENTS...

It's too difficult to master...

We don't want to make mistakes...

THAT'S TOO BIG A CHANGE...

The market is not ready yet...

SINCE WHEN ARE YOU THE EXPERT?...

It is just like...

Let's keep it under consideration...

GET REAL...

It's not my responsibility...

The older generation will not use it...

WE ARE TOO SMALL FOR THAT...

It might work in other places but not here...

There are no staff members available...

That's for the future...

Source:
Creativity Today,
Igor Byttebier
R Ramon Vullings,
BIS Publishers, 2007, p 29.
Download a poster at:
www.ideakillers.net.

Robin Williams'
character in
Dead Poets Society

No matter
tells you,
can change

what anybody words and ideas the world.

Great Ideas Have the X Factor

Everybody knows the television show where a jury looks for talent with the X factor, that "certain something" that makes for star quality. As innovators, we are also in search of ideas with the X factor. But when do our ideas have it? Which criteria must an idea meet to give it star quality?

Generally in this early phase, an idea is little more than a fleeting thought, a word or image whereby we experience a mild 'we-have-to-do-something-with-this' sensation. It is only a rough diamond, like most candidates in the first round of the X factor. And there is still a long way to go. An important question is, is it enough to survive the corporate innovation jury?

An idea with the X factor is very appealing to (new) customers, very appealing to your company and can be brought to life quickly. In my own innovation practice, these three core qualities lead to seven characteristics for great ideas for innovative products, services or business models:

1. Very appealing to customers.
2. It stands out in the market.
3. It has great potential for extra turn-over.
4. It has adequate profit potential.
5. It fits management's business goals.
6. It is (somehow) considered quickly feasible.
7. It creates its own internal support.

It is pretty evident that potential customers have to see the new product idea as something really attractive. During the innovation process, customers can serve as a fanbase, similar to the viewers of the X-factor shows while the idea is still being developed.

However, there is more to it than that. The new product or service idea must really stand out in the market and supply concrete advantages relevant to the current situation of customers (a camera tablet for the inspection of the small intestine). It must give potential customers a concrete reason to change. A really innovative product or service idea will solve relevant problems of customers (long lasting flowers), or will make something totally new possible (Virgin Galactic space flights). This not only applies to the consumer market, but also to B2B markets where services or products often play a huge role in the business processes of customers. When it comes to the decision to buy, many people and departments are involved. There will have to be a definite reason to consider changing to something new (Tarmac that can be rolled up like a carpet saves a lot of time to apply).

An attractive and distinctive new product idea might cause a stir internally. It is therefore important that you are fully aware of possible resistance from the start. There's often more than one X factor jury member who has a different opinion. Manfred Kets de Vries, professor in management and leadership at INSEAD, once said: 'The only person waiting for a change is a baby with a wet diaper.' He is spot on with this. An idea must fit your personal goal as a manager for it to get your support. Companies look for fast growth. It's an idea with the X factor if it will bring higher turnover and more profits and, above all, if it is somehow considered to be feasible in the short term.

So, to reach the X factor finals, an innovative idea must successfully pass through a lot of stations in the innovation process. Ideally, a good new product idea is not only supported by the creators, but must eventually have gained the full support of the development team, senior management as well as line management, even if there was some opposition at the beginning.

A good idea may not be obvious to everyone right away. It may look and sound like Susan Boyle, the Scottish singer discovered on *Britain's got Talent*, April 2009. Global interested was sparked by the huge contrast between her powerful voice and her plain appearance on stage. Within nine days of her audition, videos of Boyle had been viewed over 100 million times.[1]

1. Source: Wikipedia.

DIVERGE

CONVERGE

1. INTRODUCE

2. INSPIRE

3. GENERATE IDEAS

> 500

30-40

4. GROUP AND CHOOSE IDEA DIRECTIONS

12

5. PRODUCE IDEA MINDMAPS

12

6. PRODUCE INNOVATIVE CONCEPTS

7. PRESENT CONCEPTS

8. EVALUATE INNOVATIVE CONCEPTS

9. WRAP UP

STRUCTURED BRAINSTORMING

25 RULES
FOR PERFECT BRAINSTORMING

Every one of us has experienced failed brainstorming sessions. It could have been because one of your vice presidents disapproved of every idea until after a short while everybody kept his mouth shut. Or because 250 ideas were posted on a wall and nobody knew what move to take next. Or because at the end of a long day at the office you could only recycle old ideas and nothing new was unveiled. But do not get discouraged. The perfect brainstorm does exist – just like the perfect storm.

So, what finally gives that feeling of WOW? I've discovered that this simple question cannot be answered easily. I do not think there is one dominant success factor. It is much more the right interplay of many small factors. It's all in the details. Perhaps the metaphor of a puzzle is most fitting. There are many small pieces needed, and if you lose one, the puzzle is worthless. In my innovation practice, I have found 25 pieces needed to create perfect brainstorming:

HIGHLY RELEVANT

1. Define a relevant subject, which is a challenge for the organization and the people you invite.
2. Create with the sponsor a concrete and s.m.a.r.t. brainstorming or innovation assignment.
3. Create momentum for brainstorming. Something important must happen now!

DIVERSE GROUP OF PARTICIPANTS

4. Invite people for whom the assignment is personally relevant.
5. Invite people for both content as well as decision-making capabilities.
6. Include outsiders and outside-the-box thinkers.
7. Include an even mix of men and women, young & old, et cetera.
8. Invite the internal senior problem-owner (CEO or vice president) to participate.

SPECIAL SETTING

10. Create an (emotionally) safe environment where you can be yourself.
11. Don't allow iPhones and iPads to ring or flash.
12. Never - and I really mean never do any brainstorming at the office.

FACILITATED BY A PROFESSIONAL

21. Appoint an (internal) expert facilitator, who stays in the background and exercises light control.
22. The facilitator should reflect the opposite energy of the group. If the group is too active: exert calmness.
23. The facilitator mustn't lose sight of subgroups; closely monitor their progress.

EFFECTIVELY STRUCTURED PROCESS

13. Allow at least two days for effective brainstorming to reach concrete new concepts.
14. Spend twice as much time on the convergence process as on the divergence process.
15. Plan and prepare an effective combination of idea-generating techniques.
16. Be open to suggestions from the group to adapt the process.
17. Make sure it is enjoyable. Fun promotes good results.
18. Time box. Make sure everybody is aware of the time limits- and sticks to them.
19. Hire a storyboard artist or cartoonist to visualize the results
20. Keep up the pace; otherwise it becomes long-winded and boring.

CONCRETE OUTPUT

24. Make the output very concrete and clear to anybody.
25. Creating concepts together with your colleagues generates maximum internal support.

THE ORIGIN OF

Ben Cohen and Jerry Greenfield grew up in Merrick, Long Island, U.S.A. They became friends in junior high school. Jerry finished college, but wasn't accepted into any med schools. Ben got into several colleges, but ended up dropping out of all of them. They soon realized that doing what they were doing wasn't getting them anywhere. That is when they decided to start their own business.

However, neither of them had any experience starting a business. But they did know what they liked and that was food- especially ice cream. So it seemed like a logical step to open an ice cream shop. To get started, they followed a $5 correspondence course on ice cream-making from Penn State University. They then combined their $8000 life savings with a $4000 bank loan and took out a lease on an old gas station building in Burlington, Vermont. They opened for business on May 5, 1978. Using an old-fashioned ice cream freezer, they began churning out all the 'rich & creamy', 'fun & chunky' ice cream flavors they'd always dreamed about. Flavors loaded with all their favorite chunks of fruits, nuts, candies, and cookies. They started with 12 flavors. Soon there were long lines of customers outside the old gas station. Their ice cream was a hit. In the summer of 1978, Ben & Jerry launched their first creative initiative that would help expand their company by holding a free summer film festival. They projected films onto a bare wall of their building. By 1980, Ben & Jerry had begun selling their ice cream to numerous restaurants in the Burlington area. Ben drove an old VW bus delivering their ice cream products to customers. On his delivery route, he passed many small grocery and convenience stores. He decided that they would be a perfect outlet for their ice cream. In 1980, they rented space in an old spool and bobbin factory in Burlington and began packaging their ice cream in pint-size cartons with pictures of themselves on the package. Ben & Jerry's first gained national

BEN & JERRY'S

attention in the U.S.A. in 1981 when *Time* magazine named their products as 'the best ice cream in the world' in a cover story. In the following year, Ben & Jerry's began to expand its distribution beyond the state of Vermont. First, an out-of-state store selling Ben & Jerry's products opened in Portland, Maine. Then, the company began to sell its pints in the Boston area, distributing their goods to stores through independent channels.

With its continuing expansion, Ben & Jerry's developed a need for tighter financial controls. They brought in a local nightclub owner, Fred 'Chico' Lager, with business experience to be chief operating officer. As sales grew sharply, Ben Cohen and Jerry Greenfield slowly came to the realization that their small-scale business had far-exceeded their expectations. This unexpected success didn't entirely please them. 'When Jerry and I realized we were no longer ice cream men, but businessmen, our first reaction was to sell."

Together with their employees, Ben Cohen and Jerry Greenfield drafted a three-part mission statement summing up the company's unique corporate philosophy. It declared that Ben & Jerry's had a product mission, a social mission, and an economic mission. In their pursuit of developing innovative ways to improve the quality of life for a broad community, they launched flavors such as 'Chocolate Fudge Brownie', containing brownies made by

homeless and unemployed workers in Yonkers, New York; 'Wild Maine Blueberry', made with blueberries harvested by Passamaquoddy Indians; and 'Rainforest Crunch', containing Brazil nuts collected in the Amazon rainforest by indigenous natives. In addition, 60 percent of the profits from that flavor were invested in environmental groups dedicated to preserving the Amazon rainforest. Initiatives such as these provide an economically viable alternative to deforestation.

When confronted with a declining market for super premium ice cream, Ben Cohen and Jerry Greenfield turned increasingly to professional managers. Finally in April 2000, Unilever acquired Ben & Jerry's, its only super premium ice cream, for $326 million in cash. Unilever, pledging to uphold Ben & Jerry's traditional values and commitment to social causes, offered the power to distribute Ben & Jerry's to millions of new consumers; expanding the Ben & Jerry's brand to new heights.

Source: www.benjerry.com. www.fundinguniverse.com/company-histories/ben-jerry-s-homemade-inc-history/ www.wikipedia.org. www.entrepreneur.com/article/197626.

VI.

Test Ideas

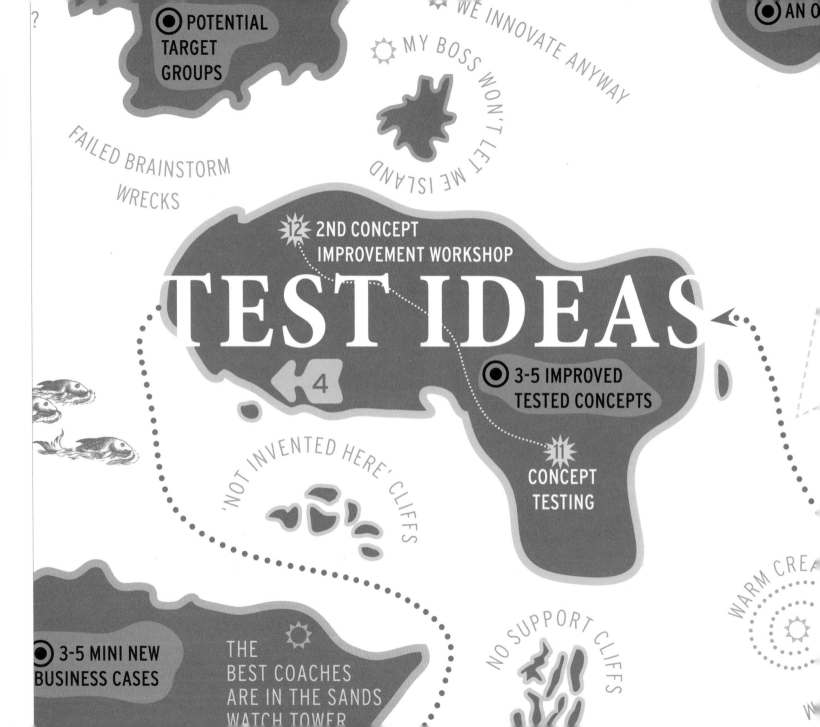

POTENTIAL TARGET GROUPS

MY BOSS WON'T LET ME ISLAND

WE INNOVATE ANYWAY

AN O

FAILED BRAINSTORM WRECKS

12 2ND CONCEPT IMPROVEMENT WORKSHOP

TEST IDEAS

4

3-5 IMPROVED TESTED CONCEPTS

'NOT INVENTED HERE' CLIFFS

11 CONCEPT TESTING

WARM CREA

3-5 MINI NEW BUSINESS CASES

THE BEST COACHES ARE IN THE SANDS WATCH TOWER

NO SUPPORT CLIFFS

STEP 4: TEST IDEAS

How attractive are the new concepts and how many truly stand out? Let's reflect on this together with customers and improve the concepts based on their feedback. Test Ideas takes three weeks and is the fourth step of the ideation phase.

How attractive are the new product concepts? You have created them yourself which naturally makes you extremely enthusiastic about them. However, it´s smart to get the customer's opinion as well. This way you´ll receive useful feedback about the clarity of the new concepts, which can be helpful in improving them. The attractiveness is directly tested on the target group. Qualitative concept research can be performed quickly on a small scale and simultaneously in different countries or continents. The indicative character of the research is not an issue as concepts will be tested on a larger scale further down in the regular product development process. Right now, the main reason for the concept research is to gain insight into why customers are or are not attracted to the new product concept.

For concept testing in the B2B target groups, individual in-depth interviews are preferred. There is greater confidentiality and more open feedback. The new concepts are presented one by one to individual respondents during the interview. This can be done at the customer's work place or in a research room. Focus groups of six to eight people are an excellent form of testing new consumer products, services and business models. A good independent market researcher will not allow individual opinions to be outweighed by the few extroverts, who can always be found in a group. If possible, core team members are present at the research venue. This has the advantage that it will help members find new inspiration and make immediate improvements. Online concept testing is an excellent alternative for 'live' concept testing for concepts intended to be introduced internationally or globally.

During the qualitative concept research, negative aspects are also pointed out. This might be hard to take, but that is, after all, what the research is meant to uncover.

The first responses of potential customers on the concepts offer wonderful input for the team. Therefore, a concept improvement workshop is organized directly following the concept testing. The results of the concept research are presented during this second concept improvement workshop. In a brainstorming session all team members work together on finding ways to adjust the negative aspects. At the end of this improvement workshop it is decided which three to five concepts will be developed into mini new business cases in the next step. Also, the chosen concepts are matched together with core team members, working in pairs, who will be responsible for its development.

At the end of the fourth step, the ideation team has tested twelve new concepts of which three to five are chosen to be developed into mini new business cases.

GO TO THE FORTH WEBSITE AND DOWNLOAD THE FOUR PRACTICAL CHECKLISTS OF THE STEP TEST IDEAS
(www.forth-innovation.com/forth-steps/test-ideas/)

FACTSHEET   STEP 4

Duration	3 weeks
Activities	11. Concept Testing 12. Second Concept Improvement Workshop
Deliverables	Three to five improved tested concepts
Outcome	Three to five improved tested concepts that will be developed into mini new business cases.
Crucial moments	1. The opinion of the customer is the moment of truth. 2. Which three to five concepts are chosen to be worked out as mini new business cases in the final step? 3. Which core team duo will work out which mini new business case?
Risks	1. Do we get enough customers with the right profile to participate in the concept test? 2. Does everyone show up at the concept test? 3. Customers in the test don't appreciate any of the concepts. How do we continue?
Next step	Homecoming: Three to five concepts are developed into mini new business cases and adopted by the organization for development.

TIPS FOR NEW CONCEPT TESTING

1. The qualitative element

The purpose of concept research is to test if the newly developed product concepts are attractive to the target group.

Are you on the right track? In addition to the testing aspect, the final stages of this research also contain quite a bit of exploratory elements. It's much more than a simple "yah" or "nay". Above all, it's about understanding the current behavior and preferences of the target group that could explain the group members' reaction to new concepts. Why do they have the opinions that they have? Furthermore, you also want to find concrete points of reference to improve the developed concepts.

2. Method and criteria of product concepts

- Small scale and indicative.
- Preferably carry out the research with: prototypes, three-dimensional designs or detailed sketches of products; or practical descriptions of services.
- Preferably conduct the research with people in actual user situations:
  Discuss product concepts for new beers in a bar.
  Discuss new catering concepts in a company restaurant.
  Discuss new household appliances in a kitchen.
  This is a bit more difficult for services. You can use research rooms for this.

3. Questionnaire

Draft a questionnaire together with experienced in-depth interviewers from the agency. You can use the following types of questions (make them specific for your sector and target group):

- Exploratory:
  - What is the current purchasing and usage behavior? (Why?)
  - What are the major purchasing motivations? (Why?)
  - What are you currently using? (Why?)
  - What do you like about the current products on the market? (Why?)
  - What don't you like? (Why?)
- Testing:
  - Do you recognize the customer friction? (Why?)
  - Is the concept clear? (Why?)
  - Is it relevant to you? (Why?)
  - Is it attractive? (Why?)
  - Does it distinguish itself? (Why?)
  - Does it fit the brand? (Why?)
  - Do you consider it credible? (Why?)
  - Is it something for you? (Why?)
  - Would you buy it? (Why?)
  - How much do you think it will cost? (Why?)
  - Would you have anything about it changed? (Why?)

4. Target group

Choose a conversation partner from the target group described in your innovation assignment.

Tip: stick to this!

5. Participants involved in the ideation team

- Invite all core team members (and the extended team members) to be present.
- Mindset: ask the team members to observe and listen closely to the responses given in the interviews. This is how they will be inspired for possible improvements.
- Ensure that core team members are present in all countries for the qualitative research.

6. Choosing the agency

- There are many good qualitative interviewers and market research agencies. Look for people with a lot of experience conducting in-depth interviews, preferably with experience in the relevant product group or sector.
- There are international networks of qualitative research agencies. Seek out the networks that truly share the same vision, use the same methods and have branches in all the countries. When you need to test for B2B concepts, seek out the agencies that are specialized in this.

Tip: Record the interviews. The client feedback can then be referred back to later in FORTH or in the product development process. For instance, to show management or the product development team how positive or critical the target audience was regarding a specific new product concept.

Steve Jobs, businessman:

You can't just what they want give that to them. get it built, something ask customers and then try to By the time you they'll want new.

TESTING A NEW CONCEPT

Please circle to which extent the concepts meet the following five criteria.

1. Recognition
Do you recognize the customer situation and friction, mentioned in the beginning?

2. Clear
Is the concept clear to you?

3. Attractive
Is the concept attractive to you?

1. No, not at all
2.
3.
4.
5. Yes, 100 percent

1. No, not at all
2.
3.
4.
5. Yes, 100 percent

1. No, not at all
2.
3.
4.
5. Yes, 100 percent

IN 5 QUESTIONS

4. Fits the brand
Does the concept fit the brand mentioned?

5. Buy
Are you interested in buying the concept?

Grade this concept
on a scale from 1-10
(1 = very poor & 10 = excellent)

1. No, not at all
2.
3.
4.
5. Yes, 100 percent

1. No, not at all
2.
3.
4.
5. Yes, 100 percent

Positive aspects:

Negative aspects:

Suggestions for improvement:

What a Brilliant Idea!

What a brilliant idea! That's what a lot of people think after a new idea pops into their minds. Or it's something someone said at the end of a wonderful two-day ideation workshop where a team of colleagues has just brainstormed a lot of new concepts. Of course, at that very moment it looks and feels like utter brilliance. Just like adoring parents swooning over their child. But, in this instance is it really justified?

Well actually, most new ideas don't lead to new successful products. There is considerable evidence that shows of the thousands of ideas out there, only one of them is converted into to a successful product. It takes 3,000 raw ideas to get to 1 successful product.[1] Many ideas cannot be transformed into products due to technical or economic reasons or because customers are not interested.

So brilliant new ideas require three checks:
1. Customer: will it be liked?
2. Business model: will it be profitable?
3. Technology: will it be feasible?

A lot of ideas are generated from an ideation workshop, idea contest or R&D and marketing getting together. Therefore, it's wise to first do a quick-and-dirty check on all three aspects. In my innovation practice, I notice most companies check the feasibility. Some of them also check the viability of the business model. But hardly anyone checks if the customers will like the idea at the front end of the innovation process. Why do organizations forget to connect with customers at the front end of innovation?

- Arrogance: we know what's best for them;
- Ignorance: we didn't give it any thought;
- Habit: this is not something we've ever done;
- Laziness: this is a lot of hassle;
- Fear of rejection: they will criticize us;
- Fear of openness: they will steal the idea from us;

Having been involved in a lot of early concept testing, one thing strikes me most. In almost every innovation project, the ranking of top ideas made by the innovation team was completely different from the ranking made by their customer focus groups.

You are absolutely right to fear that your customers will criticize your ideas. That is exactly what they do. And that is the one reason testing your 'brilliant' ideas out on customers has such a great added value. In an era where the speed to market is increasingly more important, you shouldn't waste valuable time and resources on hopeless concepts. Quit as early as possible and focus your attention on developing products or services with a promising concept and good market perspective. This will boost your innovation productivity and reduce the time to market.

Connect customers early in your product development process and check if customers will like the product a.s.a.p.

1. Stevens, G.A. and J. Burley, "3000 Raw Ideas = 1 Commercial Success!", May/June 1997, Research Technology Management, Vol 40, #3, pp. 16-27.

A PERFECT NEW CONCEPT

In my practice as an innovation specialist, I developed a practical checklist to verify new concepts. It lists ten criteria which a new concept must meet if it is ever to become successful. Five of these criteria are from the perspective of the customer. The other five are from the perspective of the organization. It's easy to implement. Use it in practice for your own innovation.

Customer's perspective:
1. Is it relevant for the customer?
2. Is the solution superior on a relevant aspect?
3. Is its uniqueness easy to explain to the customer?
4. Is it easy for the customer to try?
5. Can the customer change to our concept without any risk?

Organization's perspective:
6. Does it have the required potential in turnover and profits?
7. Can it be done without directly competing with our other products or services?
8. Does it fit our brand positioning?
9. Can we make it (with the help of partners)?
10. Can it be done without huge investments?

If the answer is 'yes' to all ten questions, your concept is a no-brainer; just do it! If not, take time to pause and rethink your strategy.

1.   CHANGE VOICE TAPE @ SUNSE

NIGHT PASS:

PILOT:

1.   ROUTE UMBILICAL THROUGH U
      GUIDE
2.   POSITION FEET IN FOOT RES
      (PRIOR TO SUNSET)
      SUNSET @ 55:00 ET OR 43:3
3.   INSTALL ADAPTER WORK STAT
      CAMERA (CONNECT PWR CABLE

CMD PILOT:

1.   EVA CAMERA C/B - CLOSED
2.   EVA CAMERA PWR SWITCH - (

PILOT:

1.   START CAMERA (VERIFY CAM
2.   REST
3.   PULL UMBILICAL TAUT & IN:
      CLIP ON HAND BAR
4.   UNSTOW AND POSITION MIRR
5.   UNSTOW PEN LIGHTS, ACTUA
      LIGHTS TO HAND BARS WITH
6.   EVALUATE FOOT RESTRAINTS
7.   REST
8.   PERFORM WORK STATION TAS
                  ADAPTER
      A.   PERFORM THE FOLLOWIN
            FOOT RESTRAINTS:
            1.   OPEN POUCH AND R
                  WRENCH
            2.   PERFORM TORQUEIN

		7.	CUT 2 STRANDS OF RIGHT SIDE OF ELECTRICAL CABLE & FLUID QD CABLE	
ICAL		8.	STOW CUTTERS IN POUCH	
		9.	REMOVE PIP-PINS FROM HAND HOLDS AND STOW	
NTS		10.	UNSTOW WRENCH FROM VELCRO & REMOVE SATURN BOLT. STOW WRENCH ON VELCRO	
G.E.T.		11.	ATTACH WAIST TETHERS TO FIXED RINGS ON WORK STATION; REMOVE FEET FROM FOOT RE-STRAINTS	
		12.	REMOVE WRENCH FROM VELCRO & REPLACE SATURN BOLT. (ALLOW ONE MINUTE TO START BOLT) STOW WRENCH ON VELCRO /IN POUCH	
ETTING)		13.	EVALUATE HOOK & RING CON-NECTIONS	
IN		14.	REST (2 MIN)	20:(
		15.	PULL NYLON VELCRO STRIPS & RESTOW (LEFT SIDE)	
ATTACH RO		16.	PULL STEEL VELCRO STRIPS & RESTOW (RIGHT SIDE)	
		17.	DISCONNECT & CONNECT CENTER CONNECTOR	
52:00		18.	DISCONNECT & CONNECT L/H (R/H) CONNECTOR	
KS IN		19.	REPOSITION FEET IN FOOT RESTRAINTS	
ELSS HI		20.	REST (2 MIN)	25:(
RA-TOR		21.	CONNECT WAIST TETHER TO HAND HAND HOLDS & SECURE HAND HOLDS TO CHESTPACK	

Woody Allen,
film director: *If you're not
and again, it's a
doing anything*

failing every now sign you're not very innovative.

MUSEUM OF INNOVATION FAILURES

Producing failures is an essential part of innovation. It is the way we learn. Here are 10 famous innovation failures meant to intrigue you.

1. FORD EDSEL (1957)

The Edsel was cursed by a number of factors. The Edsel, also known as the 'Titanic of Automobiles', had a name that just didn't resonate with the general public, a bizarre pricing strategy, and was launched during a national recession. Only 64,000 models were sold in the U.S.A in the first year.

2. SONY BETAMAX (1979)

The 1979 Betamax was a real breakthrough for its time and for the video recording business. Despite having higher quality (and a cooler name), Betamax was defeated by VHS when over forty companies decided to use the VCR-compatible format instead.

3. COLGATE KITCHEN ENTREES (1982)

Colgate (yes, the toothpaste brand) thought it wise to launch a line of frozen dinners. Consumers could eat a Colgate meal and then brush their teeth with Colgate toothpaste. The product was a complete bust, and pulled from the shelves shortly after.

4. NEW COKE (1985)

New Coke was the reformulation of Coca-Cola. There was nothing wrong with old Coke. The public's reaction to the change was negative. The subsequent reintroduction of Coke's original formula, re-branded as "Coca-Cola Classic", was a great success.

5. PREMIER SMOKELESS CIGARETTES (1988)

By 1988, second-hand smoke was recognized as a serious health risk by a majority of the public. RJ Reynolds, the producer of Camel cigarettes, introduced Premier, a smokeless cigarette. Users complained that smoking a Premier cigarette produced an awful taste and smell.

6. THE NEWTON OF APPLE (1993)

Apple released a handheld device they hoped would change personal computing. It was officially called MessagePad. It was overpriced ($700-1000) and clunky.

8. BIC WOMEN'S UNDERWEAR (1998)

Disposability is the core of the BIC brand. BIC also applied this core concept to women's underwear, introducing 'disposable pantyhose'. After failing to attract customers, the line itself was disposed.

9. THE ZUNE OF MICROSOFT (2006)

The Zune was Microsoft's "me too" answer to the iPod. While it had some nifty product features that the iPod lacked (like sharing music from player to player), the Zune, despite an expensive marketing effort by Microsoft, never really caught on.

10. COCAINE® ENERGY DRINKS (2006)

A Las Vegas company launched an energy drink called Cocaine. It contained three times the caffeine of Red Bull and it made no apologies for its shameless brand strategy. Its marketing language was rife with drug references. Not long after its launch, the FDA pulled the drink from store shelves.

7. HARLEY DAVIDSON PERFUME (1994)

Harley Davidson has strong brand values like being "masculine, macho and a rebel". In the eyes of a lot of fans they overstretched the brand with aftershave perfumes.

Sources: 1. Wikipedia.org.
2. www.growthink.com, '10 Famous Product Failures And the Advertisements That Did Not Sell Them', Andrew Bordeaux, December 17, 2007.
3. www.saleshq.monster.com, the 20 worst product failures, Zac Frank and Tania Khadder.
4. www.dailyfinance.com/photos/top-25-biggest-product-flops-of-all-time.

THE ORIGIN OF

Twitter is an online service for social networking and microblogging that enables its users to send and read text-based messages of up to 140 characters, known as 'tweets'. Unregistered users can read tweets, while registered users can post tweets through the website interface, SMS, or a range of apps for mobile devices. Since its launch, Twitter has become one of the ten most visited websites on the Internet, and has been described as "the SMS of the Internet."

Twitter was created in San Francisco in March 2006 by Jack Dorsey of the podcasting company called Odeo. The company was facing enormous competition from Apple and other industry heavyweights and was compelled to reinvent itself. Odeo started with a series of daylong brainstorming sessions before breaking off into teams to discuss their best ideas. Dorsey was central to the Twitter team. It is widely acknowledged that it was Dorsey's idea that originally sparked Twitter. Years before Dorsey joined Odeo, he had made drawings of something resembling Twitter. Dorsey's idea was to make the service so simple that you don't even think about what you're doing, you just type something and send it: "I want to have a dispatch service that connects us on our phones using text." Dorsey's first use case was San Francisco-related: telling people that the club where he was 'is happening'. In February 2006, Noah Glass, Jack Dorsey, and Florian Weber presented Dorsey's idea to the rest of the company: a system where you could send a text to one number and it would be broadcast to all of your friends via a platform called Twttr; which later became Twitter.

By March 2006, Odeo had a Twitter prototype up and running. In August of that year, earthquake tremors were felt in San Francisco and the news spread quickly via Twitter. For users and company-watchers alike this was an early 'Aha!' moment. Then, the following month in September 2006, Odeo's CEO Evan Williams wrote a letter to Odeo's investors telling them that the company was going nowhere. He proposed to buy back the investors' shares so they wouldn't take a loss. Williams stated the following about Twitter:
"By the way, Twitter (http://twitter.com), which you may have read about, is one of the pieces of value that I see in Odeo, but it's much too early to tell what's there. Almost two months after launch, Twitter has less than 5,000 registered users. I will continue to invest in Twitter, but it's hard to say it justifies the venture investment Odeo certainly holds – especially since that investment was for a different market altogether."

TWITTER

Source: Wikipedia. The Real History of *Twitter*, Nicholas Carlson, www.businessinsider.com, April 13, 2011. How *Twitter* was Born, January 30, 2009, www.140characters.com.

follow us on
twitter

Williams eventually bought the company – and Twitter. It is estimated that the original Odeo investors sold for approximately $5 million. Multiple investors, who had combined to put $5 million into Odeo, say that William's buyout made them whole. Five years later in 2011, the assets of Twitter were estimated at least 1000 x more: $5 billion.

The twitter project team went on to win the South by Southwest Web Award of 2007 in the category 'blog'. In their famous acceptance speech they said playfully: "We'd like to thank you in 140 characters or less. And we just did!'

Since its launch in 2006, Twitter rapidly gained worldwide popularity, with over 500 million registered users as of 2012, generating over 340 million tweets daily and handling over 1.6 billion search queries per day.

VII.

Homecoming

'CUSTOMERS DON'T LIKE IT' BAY

'NOT INVENTED HERE' CLIFFS

4

THE
BEST COACHES
ARE IN THE SANDS
WATCH TOWER

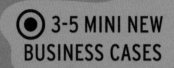◉ 3-5 MINI NEW
BUSINESS CASES

15 CONCEPT TRANSFER WORKSHOP

HOMECOMING

5

14 FINAL
PRESENTATION

13 4 MINI NEW BUSINESS
CASE WORKSHOPS

'WE CAN D
MIST

◉ AN
INNOVATIVE
MINDSET

◉ AN EFFECTIVE
IDEATION PROCESS

STEP 5: HOMECOMING

In the final step, the FORTH expedition returns home with three to five attractive new product or service concepts and enough support to fill the innovation pipeline. Homecoming is the climatic step of the 20-week expedition.

FORTH Activity 13:
Four Mini New Business Case Workshops
Working in core team duos, the best concepts are worked out as mini new business cases in four full-day workshops. It is important that the concepts presentations are convincing and easy to relate to. One excellent way, which is commonly used in the Anglo-Saxon business world, is the business case: a clear, commercial, professional and financial base for new initiatives or new investments. I call it the mini new business case; 'mini' because in this phase, its development is still only superficial. 'New', to distinguish it is a business case regarding a new concept rather than, for example, an investment. The advantage of drafting mini new business cases is that it makes every team member aware that alongside creative aspects, the commercial, professional and financial aspects also aid senior management in their decision to adopt the new concepts for further development in the innovation process. In addition,

it strengthens the concepts, as they are based on strategic, commercial, technical and financial indicators.

FORTH Activity 14:
Final Presentation
It is very important to get everyone who has not been working closely with the FORTH innovation method, enthusiastic about the concepts. An outside-the-box presentation of the FORTH expedition, in the form of a guided tour in their own 'innovation room', is usually a good way to get everyone involved. Next, it is important to present the mini new business cases to the senior managers who make the official decision whether or not to develop a product.

FORTH Activity 15:
Concept Transfer Workshop
The ideation phase ends with the admission of the new product concepts into the regular development process. In larger organizations a new team is set up for the product development phase as it requires

different skills and abilities. I strongly suggest that the development team is given access to the knowledge and expertise gained from the creation and development of the product concept. It is also advisable to allow a few participants of the ideation team to continue on working as part of the development team as this team is now responsible for the realization of the concept. These participants already know the history and origin of the concept and know which characteristics played a decisive role in the selection of these products. Their role in the development team is to safeguard the essence of the concept. So, after the decision has been made to develop a new product concept, a transfer workshop can be organized to transfer responsibility from the ideation team to the development team as well as to secure the integrity of the concept.

Homecoming takes about four weeks. The expedition ends there with three to five attractive new product or service concepts with internal support for development.

GO TO THE FORTH WEBSITE AND DOWNLOAD THE FOUR PRACTICAL CHECKLISTS OF THE STEP HOMECOMING (www.forth-innovation.com/forth-steps/) homecoming/

FACTSHEET STEP 5

Duration	4 weeks
Activities	13. Four Mini New Business Case Workshops 14. Final Presentation 15. Concept Transfer Workshop
Deliverables	Three to five mini new business cases
Outcome	Once the green light is given, three to five mini new business cases (MNBC) are developed as full new business cases (for new services and business models) or prototypes (for new products). Armed with the mini new business cases every team member returns enriched with an innovative mindset.
Crucial moments	1. Are the MNBC teams fully committed to their business cases? 2. Will the MNBCs be attractive and feasible? 3. What is the first feedback from the decision makers? 4. What fate do the decision makers choose for the MNBCs? 5. Starting follow-up development projects. 6. Transfer insights and concepts to the next teams.
Risks	1. An MNBC team doesn't get along so well together 2. An MNBC team is not fully committed to a mini new business case. 3. The calculations and estimates in the mini new business case are questionable. 4. The decision makers' response is very cautious. 5. The decision to transform the MNBCs into follow-up development projects takes a long time. 6. It takes a long time before the follow-up project is staffed, financed and set to go. 7. The insights and results of the FORTH project team are heavily discussed in the new follow-up team.
Next step	The ideation phase ends with the admission of the new product concepts into the regular development process

T. S. Eliot, poet: *The journey*

not the arrival

matters.

How to Pick the Right Idea?

Think different. That's the essence of the creative processes in coming up with ideas for innovative products, services or business models. An awful lot of brainstorming sessions or ideation workshops take place to generate fresh, new ideas. After generating ideas you end up with a wall of ideas. This is a great thing! I like to quote the American chemist and Nobel Prize winner Linus Pauling, who said "the best way to have a good idea is to have lots of ideas."

Generating 'outside the box' ideas is often not the problem in an ideation workshop with 10 or more people. The real critical moment is when you go from the divergence phase into the convergence phase. Imagine you have a wall of 500+ ideas in front of you. Now what do you do? How do you pick the right idea? That's the question.

I've spent the last 10 years experimenting a lot on how to deal with this essential question. It's not an easy one to answer. Unfortunately, I have not found the 'holy grail'. However, the great advantage of continuous experimentation in converging, selecting and improving ideas is that you do end up learning a lot. And I'd like to share five of my key learning tips on how to pick the right idea.

1. Take your time. One of the most frequent mistakes is spending a lot of time generating ideas, leaving hardly any time in the ideation workshop to converge, select and improve them. You should spend at least 2/3 of your process on picking the right idea and 1/3 on getting a lot of ideas, instead of the other way around. Promising ideas at the front end of innovation are like rough diamonds, which look like other ordinary stones, but have the potential to shine beautifully in the end. You have to take your time to be able to recognize them. And be sure to converge in several steps. Even in several workshops. Don't expect to recognize rough diamonds among 500 other stones in one or two hours.

2. Have a clear vision of what you want.
How can you select ideas if you don't know what you are looking for? Especially when the converging, selecting and improving is done as a group it is important that you have a shared vision on where you want to go. That's why it is essential to start an innovation project with a clear and concrete innovation assignment and involve your senior managers. This forces your company's senior management, from the start, to be concrete about the market/target group for which the innovations must be developed and which criteria these new concepts must meet. Use these concrete criteria to help you identify and select the right ideas in your ideation workshops.

3. Reflect from the customer's perspective.
In converging, selecting and improving ideas it is very important to criticize and challenge them from different perspectives. From my own innovation practice, I've learned that there are huge differences in how people within a company perceive new ideas and how their potential customers perceive those same ideas. And that's why I advise you to incorporate idea reflection workshops with potential target groups in your ideation process. And based on their feedback proceed to pick the right ideas and improve on them

4. Make a mini new business case.
Although mood boards and concept descriptions are a good beginning, they are often too vague for managers, who think in terms of potential turnover and profit, to make their decisions on those ideas. Managers prefer business cases: a clear, strategic, commercial, professional and financial plan for a new initiative or a new investment. So, be sure at the end, you have picked ideas that are attractive and can easily be made into mini new business cases. At this stage it is just a 'preview' of the possible business case later; it isn't as detailed yet and it has more uncertainties than its 'big brother' later on in your stage-gate innovation process. This way you make your ideas more persuasive by highlighting the strategic, commercial, and professional aspects of the innovative product or service.

5. Make a feasibility road map.
Markets are changing faster than ever, shortening the product life cycles in almost every sector. In periods of economic downturn organizations on the one hand need innovative concepts more than ever and on the other hand actually cut resources for innovation, while often denying that they do. So companies need to juggle how to generate attractive, innovative ideas which at the same time are realistic and feasible in the short term. It's your challenge to pick great ideas, which combine attractiveness with feasibility. If you don't, your innovation won't make it to the market. A number of studies on new product innovation (Robert G. Cooper, 2011) showed that for every 7 new product ideas, about 4 enter development, 1.5 are launched and only 1 succeeds. These are poor odds. Improve them, and make a feasibility road map, which will support the feasibility of your innovative product or service idea.

I hope these five learning tips on how to pick the right idea will inspire you to become an even more successful innovator!

BUSINESS MODEL CANVAS

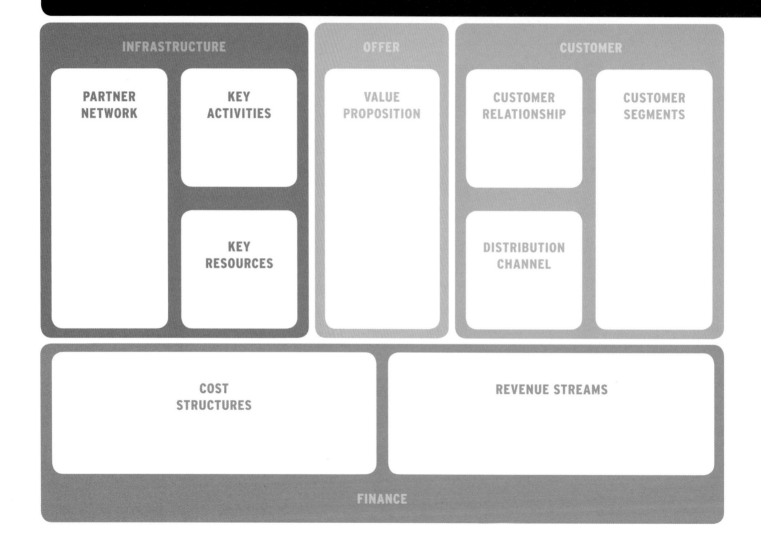

INFRASTRUCTURE

PARTNER NETWORK

KEY ACTIVITIES

KEY RESOURCES

OFFER

VALUE PROPOSITION

CUSTOMER

CUSTOMER RELATIONSHIP

CUSTOMER SEGMENTS

DISTRIBUTION CHANNEL

COST STRUCTURES

REVENUE STREAMS

FINANCE

THE BUSINESS MODEL CANVAS

(Business Model Generation, Alexander Osterwalder, Yves Pigneur, Wiley, 2010) is a management template for developing new or documenting existing business models. It is a visual chart with nine building blocks describing an organization's value proposition, infrastructure, customers and finances. A new business model starts with customer friction, i.e., any relevant need or wish from a specific customer segment that is not sufficiently satisfied. This is the basis for an innovative business model.

INFRASTRUCTURE

Key Activities: The most important activities in executing a company's value proposition.
Key Resources: The resources that are necessary to create value for the customer.
Partner Network: The partners who optimize operations and reduce risks of a business model.

CUSTOMER

Customer Segments: Various sets of customers can be segmented, based on specific needs.
Distribution Channels: Fast, efficient and cost-effective ways to deliver a company's value proposition.
Customer Relationships: The type of relationship the company wants to create with its customer segments (for example personal assistance, self-service or automated services).

OFFER

Value Propositions: The collection of products and services that serve the needs of its customers. A company's value proposition is what distinguishes the company from its competitors.

FINANCE

Cost structure: The most important financial consequences under different business models.
Revenue Streams: The way a company makes income from each customer segment.

30 Ways to Present a New Idea

There are lots of ways to present a new idea:

1. In one word.
2. With an image.
3. In a report.
4. As a mood board.
5. Do a dance.
6. Make a drawing.
7. Do a Prezi.
8. In a 140 character tweet.
9. Make a painting.
10. Make an advertising billboard.
11. Make a magazine.
12. Make a mindmap.
13. Draw a storyboard.
14. Make a statue.
15. Draw a cartoon.
16. Make a website.
17. Write one huge post-it.
18. Make a movie.
19. Make an app.
20. Sing a song.
21. Produce an advertising commercial.
22. Make a newspaper.
23. Do a flash mob on it.
24. Do a game.
25. Write a theater play.
26. Make it into a toy.
27. Present it in the form of a book.
28. Put it on a hot air balloon.
29. Put a prototype on the shelves of a regular store.
30. Make a mini new business case.

These are all wonderful presentation ideas. Most of them are very creative and outside the box. Your senior management will praise you for your creativity. But, will they buy the idea and give you the resources to develop it in the next stage? That's the question! They will evaluate your idea from at least three perspectives:

1. The Customer: will they like it?
2. The Business model: will it be profitable?
3. The Technology: will it be feasible?

That's why I am a big fan of presentation idea number 30: the mini new business case. It's a clear, strategic, commercial, professional and financial plan for a new initiative. At this stage it is more of a 'preview' of the full business case. It isn't as detailed yet and it has more uncertainties than its 'big brother' later on in your stage-gate innovation process. By making a mini new business case you strengthen the persuasiveness of your ideas by highlighting the attractiveness of the strategic, commercial, and professional aspects of the innovative product or service.

Remember: "Nobody buys from a clown."

MAGICAL IN THE FOREST

**Pat Conroy,
author:**

Once you have
voyage never ends,
over and over
quietest chambers.
never break off

traveled, the
but is played out
again in the
The mind can
from the journey.

6 MINI NEW BUSINESS CASE SHEETS

1.

THIS IS THE CUSTOMER FRICTION

2.

THIS IS OUR NEW CONCEPT

3.

THIS IS THE BENEFIT FOR THE CUSTOMER

WHAT IS THE SITUATION?

WHAT IS THE NEED?

WHAT IS THE FRICTION?

TARGET GROUP

DESCRIPTION OF THE NEW CONCEPT

NEW TO US, NEW TO THE MARKET, NEW TO THE WORLD?

NEW CONCEPT FOR AN EXISTING OR NEW MARKET?

WHY WILL THE CUSTOMER CHOOSE THIS CONCEPT?

WHO ARE OUR COMPETITORS?

WHAT'S OUR POSITIONING?

HOW WAS OUR CONCEPT RATED IN TESTS?

4.

WE CAN PRODUCE IT

FEASIBILITY

POTENTIAL PARTNERS
FOR CO-CREATION

NEXT STEPS IN THE
DEVELOPMENT PROCESS

5.

THIS IS WHAT WE GET

POTENTIAL TURNOVER

POTENTIAL MARGIN
AND PROFITS

FURTHER COSTS FOR
DEVELOPMENT

6.

WE WILL CONTINUE IN THIS WAY

WHY PROCEED?

WHAT ARE THE
UNCERTAINTIES?

NEXT STEPS:
TEAM
PLANNING
COSTS

HOW TO TRANSFER AN IDEA?

The ideation phase ends with the admission of the new product concepts into the regular development process. Larger organizations usually set up a new team for the product development phase as it requires different skills and abilities. So, how do you transfer the idea? In addition to enrolling some participants of the ideation team to continue working in the development team, it's wise to organize a:

CONCEPT TRANSFER WORKSHOP.

When?
Not too long after the ideation phase has ended.
Otherwise a lot of energy gets lost.

Duration?
Four hours.

Location?
An inspiring venue related to the new concept.

Participants?
Members of the ideation and the
development team
including the internal
client.

Program?
• Orientation.
• Goal Concept
  Transfer Workshop.
• Presentation of the new concept and Mini New Business Case.
• Presentation of major customer insights and findings during
  the ideation phase.
• Open team discussion.
• Wrap-up.

THE ORIGIN OF

Liter of Light (or Isang Litrong Liwanag) is a new global movement that aims to provide an ecologically and economically sustainable source of light to underprivileged households that do not have access to electricity or have difficulties affording electricity. The solution is a relatively simple invention. It involves filling up a 1.5L PET bottle with purified water and bleach and installing it onto the roof of a dwelling. The water inside the bottle refracts the sunlight during the daytime and creates the same luminosity as a 55-watt light bulb. With the proper installation and materials a solar bottle can last up to 5 years.

The idea of using water-filled bottles to spread daylight into dark rooms was first pioneered by the Brazilian Alfredo Moser in 2002. Students from the Massachusetts Institute of Technology (MIT) also contributed in the subsequent design and development of the technology behind Liter of Light. The students had the idea to make solar bottle bulbs when they were constructing a school classroom made out of recycled bottles in the Philippines. After construction was completed, they noticed that the school could not afford to pay the electricity bills, even though the building was sustainable. Knowing that the walls made with clear bottles let light in during the daytime, the students began experimenting with ways to use recycled bottles to bring in light through the roof.

In April 2011, Illac Diaz, founder of the MyShelter Foundation, was the first to launch a social enterprise using the Liter of Light technology in the city of Manila, Philippines. In order to help the idea to grow sustainably, the MyShelter Foundation implemented a "local entrepreneur" business model, whereby bottle bulbs are assembled and installed by locals enabling them to earn a small income. Within months, the organization expanded from one carpenter and one set of tools in one community in San Pedro, Laguna to 15,000 solar bottle bulb installations in 20 cities and provinces around the Philippines and inspired local initiatives around the world.

One year after inception, over 200,000 bottle bulbs were installed in communities around the world. Liter of Light has a goal to light up 1 million homes by the end of 2015.

Source: www.wikipedia.org. www.aliteroflight.org.

Check out this movie to see a 'liter of light' yourself!

'LITER OF LIGHT'

VIII.

Get it Done

Helpful Skills to Move Ideas into Reality

Many innovators use a phase-gated innovation process. It offers a blueprint for structuring the innovation process. A split is made between 'the fuzzy front-end' and 'the sticky back-end'. The lack of clarity in the beginning of the innovation process led to it being called the 'fuzzy front-end of innovation'. Innovation research (Cooper, 2005) reports that out of the seven new product ideas only one is successfully introduced on the market. What happened to the other six? They got stuck in the innovation delivery phase due to a lack of priority, lack of resources or because they seemed unfeasible.

So, the front-end is fuzzy and the back-end isn't very effective. Creating new products, services or business models is not easy. The fact that it is so hard is what I like about it. Learning from my 'front-end experience', I'd like to share with you three practical suggestions for the innovation delivery phase that I hope will inspire you. I call them the 3 Cs: Connect, Customer, Creativity.

Connect

Once an innovation project has passed the initial front-end gates, it becomes one of many. The big question is: how do you get your innovation project to stand out and draw the attention of the decision makers? I found a solution in the FORTH method. I have an extended team join the core project team. For the extended team I invite, on a personal basis, top decision makers from the business end of the company. The main purpose for this is to keep the members of the extended team fully aware of the progress made. And once they are made part of the team they will support the outcome. So, get top decision-makers connected to your project in the innovation delivery phase.

Customer

In innovation, the real struggle mainly lies within the organization. A lot of colleagues and managers spend their workday disagreeing on everything. In the FORTH innovation method we test twelve new product ideas among customers at the front-end. And in the last step, we focus on working out mini new business cases for the three to five most attractive concepts. We use the 'voice of the customer' to justify our choices. I suggest you continue to do the same thing at the back-end. Present your concept or prototypes to potential customers for their feedback on a regular basis. And use their enthusiasm to get higher priority and more resources internally. Use the voice of the customer!

Creativity

A lot of people associate the front-end with creativity and the back-end with structured project management. We're passed that. The front-end in the FORTH method is highly structured. And at the back-end you need more than regular project management to deliver an innovation project. Even though the soul of the innovative concept may have been created at the front-end, you'll still need to stay flexible and creative throughout the process. More than ever, you'll need professional brainstorming tools and creativity to deal with complex feasibility issues.

To help you deliver your innovation, make sure you continue using front-end ideation skills during the back-end. This will make you a much more professional innovator.

New Rules for Realizing New Ideas

Once you've got the green light from your boss, your innovation board or financer, it's once again up to you to deliver the concept you've promised them. Depending on the nature of your new concept, in the next step you will deliver a prototype, a full business case or interested business or technology partners who will join the product development team.

Naturally, you will make a delivery plan. Working at one of the large corporations you will be obliged to follow some form of project management method, like PRojects IN Controlled Environments (PRINCE). It covers the management, control and organization of a project. It tells you what you have to do to manage your projects from start to finish. It describes in-depth every step in the project life cycle, so you know exactly which tasks to complete, when and how.

The assumption is that by applying control you will reach the planned goal on time, within budget and scope. Unfortunately, you can't really call innovation a 'controlled environment'. That's why traditional project management, which puts its emphasis on heavy up-front planning, has a difficult match with innovation projects in a world which is moving faster and faster.

I hope I can provoke you into rethinking your regular approach for innovation delivery with these 11 'rules' of extreme project management[1]:

Rule 1: The management of creative people and processes calls for creative management processes.

Rule 2: The less the project manager knows about the technical issues of the project, the better.

Rule 3: What happens after the project is over is more important than what happens during the project.

Rule 4: A project plan developed without full participation of stakeholders is nothing more than one person's fantasy.

Rule 5: The more time the project manager spends with the stakeholders, the better.

Rule 6: If you haven't defined project success at the start, you'll never achieve it at the end.

Rule 7: Show them the money – nothing else matters.

Rule 8: Your project stakeholders can be your best allies or your worst enemies – you decide.

Rule 9: If you can't predict the future, don't plan it in detail.

Rule 10: If your project has not changed, be afraid – be very afraid.

Rule 11: In e-projects, a day is a lot of time.

I hope when you read this, your mind will be open to an extreme change in some of your 'regular procedures' for realizing your innovative concepts.

1. Catrine M. Jakobsen, XPM - From Idea to Realization, Synopsis, December, 2001.

Ashleigh Brilliant,
author: *Good ideas*
What's uncommon
who'll work hard

are common.
are people
enough to bring
them about.

10 PITFALLS REALIZING IDEAS

Beware!

1. Your partners don't do their job.
2. There is no business model.
3. The final product does not resemble the original.
4. The process stops for whatever reason.
5. It's not feasible.
6. Someone with the same idea is faster to market.
7. The target customer hates it.
8. Too many shortcuts were taken.
9. All the fancy names are taken.
10. You failed to market it on time.

Take Ideas to Market Faster

Shomila Malik is the Head of Enterprise Lab at Telefonica O2 UK. She has over 14 years experience in conception and delivery of creative mobile services for IBM, FT and Telefonica O2, blending business, technology, and innovation management. Rapid and collaborative innovation is her focus. The telecommunications landscape has changed. Telco providers are able to try out betas and iterate fast, even fail and be accepted.

The regular product development process is suited to traditional products. In this model, it's difficult to stop half way and change your mind – too much time, effort and cost have already been spent – even with agile development processes. For the telecommunications world, it means that every product adheres to the 'telco grade' but this whole process takes months and months. It has many dependencies – especially the suppliers who are usually other large companies with similar processes. It quickly gets complex and very difficult. Trying to innovate in this process is a challenge – too much room for distraction and too many stakeholders. A few companies succeed when they are ruthlessly focused on a product.

The Enterprise Lab is a division of the Lab at O2, which is a team that develops beta products to go to market faster. Started in January 2011, it operates in the UK – close to the market. It allows people outside O2 to try beta products, Consumer and Enterprise, under their own lab brand. Successful betas move to an industrialization path outside the lab. The management is very light. The team is about 40 people, mostly developers and there are four managers. The role of the managers involves selecting projects to work on, allocating resource to projects, working with other areas of the business to maintain good relationships with stakeholders, manage budgets, coaching and setting product strategy and goals.

The objectives are tied to those of the business but have specific targets for the lab – some objectives are based on product success and some are around people. There is a high degree of autonomy for the lab – they are able to set their own objectives and strategy. A steering committee is in place, which meets once a quarter to give feedback on their direction – it is made up of a small number of directors. The idea is that the steering committee acts as venture capitalists and the Lab tries to operate as a startup as much as possible. The O2 Enterprise Lab has focus on openness: open at the front end and in execution, open APIs, open source, and beta testing. Openness is also necessary as they let others bring the product through industrialization.

"O2 Connect": developing VoIP on mobile in four months

"In the UK, mobile coverage is not so good at home and at the office: a lot of users are going to Skype and Viber, accessing their phone over wifi in VoIP technology. Skype owns phone numbers, so you can even get called on your own phone number. We decided to explore the opportunity of competing with our own VoIP service.

We sought a specialist partner (on VoIP) because we wanted something high quality that was different – we knew we could produce something better with a niche provider rather than a large supplier who would provide the same for all telecommunications companies. We wanted

a partner who was as motivated as us – and would challenge our own thinking. By working with a small, focused partner, we could cut out dependencies, distractions and shorten the time to market. We set-up an "open innovation" collaboration with start-up Voxygen, a technology company, specialized in designing innovative communications products. Sharing product definition, leveraging on Voxygen's know-how to create open source components and acting with a similar culture, led us to great collaboration and faster development."

"O2 Connect" was delivered in four months, integrated with our network, and launched in October 2011. It won the 'highly commended' award for best new VOIP service.

"The key success factor was autonomy for the team and high level support. One of the key factors to be able to work fast is to reduce the number of decision makers so we worked in a small team and made key decisions ourselves."

Source: Taken from Nicolas Bry's interview (nbry. wordpress.com) with Shomila Malik. www.innovationexcellence.com/blog/2012/09/10/take-ideas-faster-to-market-by-shomila-malik-head-of-o2-enterprise-lab/.

THE IDEA IS READY.

WHAT'S NEXT...

Specify
Execute
Design
Develop
Deploy
Implement
Prepare
Change
Communicate
Calculate
Present
Create
Structure
Make
Explicate
Alter
Assemble
Try
Prototype
Build
Research
Produce
Test
Modify
Introduce

IX.

The
Innovation
Toolkit

THE INNOVATION TOOLKIT

This innovation toolkit lays out 37 techniques and tools for you to use in your projects at the start of innovation. Section 1 includes six openers: warm up activities to facilitate the start of a workshop. Section 2 presents three exercises to energize the group. Section 3 offers a wonderful technique to conclude a workshop. Section 4 describes thirteen idea generation tools and Section 5 provides eight tools to select and improve ideas. Sections 6 through 8 introduce three additional ways to brainstorm: playing brainstorm games, using brainstorm software and online brainstorming. Sections 9 and 10 explain two other useful techniques, the TRIZ and SIT tools, which both can be used at the start of innovation. Section 11, the final section of the toolkit ends with a technique developed by de Bono named the Six Thinking Hats.

1. OPENERS

For the effectiveness of every workshop or brainstorming session it is important that the participants feel at ease. Being made to feel safe in a group is one of many factors that contribute to getting participants to express their opinions. We are all familiar with spontaneous 'getting to know one another' encounters where each person introduces him or herself as a way of getting acquainted. The drawback to this approach is that people who don't really know each other yet, might not know what to say. Luckily, there are helpful activities that can be implemented for a smoother "getting acquainted" phase.

Below you will find an explanation of six techniques.

1.1 Photo introduction
Duration: 20 - 30 minutes

Procedure:
- Place a collection of 100 - 200 photos on one of the tables.
- The facilitator asks each person to choose a photo which says something about him or her personally.
- The participants choose one photo and return to their seats.
- The facilitator then chooses one person, someone who is an extrovert and clearly feels at ease in the group, to start his or her introduction with the help of the photo. The rest will follow suit.

Some effective alternatives can be:
- You can ask the participants beforehand to bring a photo of their own.
- In a new product brainstorming session about travel products you can ask the participants beforehand to bring a photo or other memorabilia from their favorite holiday.

1.2 Keychain introduction
Duration: 20 - 30 minutes

This technique is a nice way to get some insight into another person's life. All participants are asked to take out the keys they have with them: the key to a second home, the neighbor's key, the key to the house of a son or daughter, the office key, or simply the car key. This technique always creates humorous moments and a relaxed atmosphere; especially when everyone can relate to the person who has no idea what a specific key goes to.
A wallet can be used as an alternative.

Procedure:
- The facilitator asks the participants, to introduce themselves and tell about each key on their keychain. What kind of key is it and why do they have it?

1.3 Your innovation
Duration: 20 - 30 minutes

This technique is useful if your workshop is on innovation. You can ask the participants beforehand to bring an example of an innovation they frequently use in their personal lives. This will give you insight in their personal lives and tells you something about their personal definition of what an innovation is.

Procedure:
- The facilitator asks the participants to introduce themselves one by one and present an innovative product or service from their personal lives. What is it? Why is this innovative?

1.4 The sequence game
Duration: 10 minutes

Immediately following the introductions with the various photos, keys or wallets, the participants will proceed by playing the sequence game. The sequence game motivates the participants to quickly co-operate with each other and at the same time learn something new about one another.

Procedure:
- The facilitator asks the participants to find a space to stand in a group, and see how quickly they can work together.
- The facilitator gives instructions for the participants to perform as a group.
- The instructions could be: Stand in order of:
  - height;
  - age;
  - number of children;
  - distance from home to the brainstorming venue;
  - number of miles driven with current car.

Tip: When the participants stand in order, let them call out the numbers. By doing so, they will learn something about each other and you, as the facilitator, can monitor if the activity was done correctly.

1.5 Mix it up

It often happens that at sessions like this, the participants will go and sit next to somebody they know and, if you don't do something about it, they will consider that seat as 'theirs'. It is good to break through these patterns right away. This will speed up the process of making the external participants become part of the group. A simple rule to follow is: move your feet, lose your seat. The facilitator explains to the group that whenever someone gets up to get some coffee or post something on the ideas wall, he or she will have to take a seat somewhere else. Only apply this rule on the first morning of the first day of the brainstorming session. On the subsequent days, the group formation will make this rule unnecessary.

1.6 The trash can
Duration: 10 minutes

This is an effective technique to get participants to check their past baggage at the door and prevent it from negatively influencing the session. Participants in an innovation workshop might have had some negative experiences in the past in their organization. Perhaps their company was recently re-organized. When you, as the facilitator, see that there are factors at play that will negatively influence the brainstorming process; it is then wise to address this. It will not be possible to discuss all these negative experiences at this particular venue, but it is possible to give that negativity a place - a physical place - in the trash can.

Procedure:
- The facilitator asks the participants if they have had any recent negative experiences within their organization. They are then asked to list each of these experiences on a post-it and are given the assurance that none of these will be discussed with the group.
- The facilitator then takes a big trash bag and asks the participants to drop their post-its inside. This gives the participants a way to let go of all their negative experiences from the past.
- The facilitator closes the bag and asks someone to place it outside the room. Usually you will notice a more relaxed atmosphere as if the tension has been removed from the room.

2. ENERGIZERS

It often happens that the energy level of the group decreases at some point during the workshop as it might be mentally very tiring. If the group is up to it, interrupt the program for an energizer. The following three activities can be done.

2.1 The horse race
Duration: 10 minutes

Procedure:
- During this activity the participants pretend they are jockeys at an actual horse race track. The facilitator plays the role of the racetrack announcer. The participants are then asked to kneel in a circle close to one another. As soon as the race starts, they start tapping on the floor with their hands imitating the sound of the horses' hooves. While they continue tapping, they have to react to five commands given by the facilitator. Each command is accompanied by the following physical responses:
  - the horses are on their way - tap on the floor;
  - the horses are going through a trough of water - tap on the thigh;
  - turn to the left - everyone leans to the left;
  - turn to the right - everyone leans to the right;
  - passing the stands - everyone does the wave!

It is an art to keep it fun and to increase the tempo so that the actions steadily become faster. It is also a test of everyone's energy level, especially that of the facilitator.

2.2 Swing to the beat
Duration: 10 minutes

Procedure:
- Place the chairs to one side of the room.
- The facilitator then asks everybody to stand in the middle.
- He or she then announces that all the participants are going to move and swing to different kinds of music.
- Choose the music carefully and build it up from relaxed to fast beat. The following order is suggested: new age music, classical music, ballads, rock-and-roll and techno house. It is important that the facilitator also participates and demonstrates what to do. Some might be hesitant at first, but reassure them that anything goes; the dancing can be fast and furious or slow and relaxed.
- Be sure to increase the tempo and volume of the music and end with a grand finale.

2.3 In touch
Duration: 15 minutes

Procedure:
- Place the chairs to one side of the room.
- The facilitator asks everyone to stand in the middle.
- He or she then announces that they are going to do an exercise to get them moving. Ask everyone to wander around the room in circles; not following each other, but randomly. At the command of the facilitator everyone must walk slower or faster.
- As soon as the facilitator calls out a body part, the participants have to touch everyone they encounter with only that specific part of the body. Start with something simple, like 'hands!'. After that you can call out something less obvious, like 'the back of the head!' 'Toes!' are also nice and you can continue with 'hips!', 'noses!' and 'cheeks!'. Allow the participants to set their own boundaries.

Source: Marcel Karreman (2002). *Warming-ups & energizers*. Zaltbommel: Thema.

3. CLOSER: THE COMPLIMENT GAME

At the end of a workshop everybody is obviously tired, but above-all pleased with the group's accomplishments and the room swells with the triumph of excellence. It is meaningful to end the session with the compliment game, especially at the final meeting of a series. What makes this game so valuable is that everyone receives a personalized 'gift' to take back home: a bundle of compliments.
Duration: 20 minutes

Procedure:
- Each participant is asked to write down a compliment about the other participants. One compliment per post-it.
- Then they have to stick the post-its on the backs of the people for whom the compliments are intended. The compliment should be a word, which describes personal strengths, such as 'open', 'practical' or 'creative'.
- When this task is completed; the facilitator then asks everyone to stand in a semi-circle. You, as the facilitator, collect the post-its from the person to your left and ask him or her to read the compliments aloud. Then continuing clockwise, this person removes the notes from his or her neighbor's back and has the neighbor read this following set of compliments aloud.
- Continue until each participant has had his or her turn.
- At the end of the session, everyone has a bundle of compliments to take back home as a small gift.

Source: Mieke van de Pol.
www.decreatievetrainer.blogspot.com,
September 8, 2007.

4. IDEA GENERATION TOOLS

4.1 Brain Dump

The brain dump is the starting technique for idea generation; to unleash the first spontaneous ideas. The participants 'brain' dump whatever comes to mind first and the facilitator then harvests these ideas.
Duration: 30 - 45 minutes
(depending on the number of participants).

Procedure:
- The facilitator reads the innovation assignment and asks the participants to write down their first ideas (in a few key words) in silence on a post-it. One idea per post-it.
- The facilitator invites two participants at a time to the front of the group to read their ideas aloud, quickly one by one, and to post them on the idea wall.
- The facilitator asks the rest of the participants to listen well and write any new ideas on a post-it.
- This continues until all the participants have come to the front in pairs to read their ideas aloud before sticking their post-its onto the idea wall and there are no more ideas left.

4.2 Innovation Opportunities

In the FORTH innovation process core team members have explored innovation opportunities in step 2: Observe & Learn. These innovation opportunities are a wonderful source of inspiration for innovative ideas. Use them early in the idea generation phase.
Duration: 45 minutes
as a separate tool; 20 minutes as part of the brain dump.

Procedure A: as a separate tool:

- The inspiration of the six to ten innovation opportunities are posted on the wall.
- The facilitator asks the 'owner' of the innovation opportunity to inspire the group on what he or she has discovered and what lessons have been learned. Top innovation opportunities get three minutes to make their pitch to the group. The other innovation opportunities are only given one minute.
- Listening to the opportunities, participants are invited to jot down their ideas (in a few key words) in silence on a post-it. One idea per post-it.
- Afterwards, the facilitator invites two participants at a time to come to the front of the group to read their ideas aloud, quickly one after the other, and to post them onto the idea wall. This continues until all the participants have stuck their post-its on the wall and there are no more ideas left.

Procedure B: as part of the brain dump:

- To shorten the process, you can integrate the innovation opportunities with the ideas produced in the brain dump.
- After the participants in the brain dump have jotted down their first ideas (in a few key words) on a post-it in silence, the facilitator proceeds to facilitate the innovation opportunities tool by integrating the ideas harvested from the brain dump and the innovation opportunities in one shift. It is my experience that you will gain a lot of time, without compromising its effectiveness.

4.3 Customer Frictions

In the FORTH innovation process core team members have discovered customer frictions in step 2: Observe & Learn. Meeting customers in person and finding out the frictions of the customer are a wonderful source of inspiration for innovative ideas. Use them as innovation opportunities early on in the idea generation phase.

Duration: 45 minutes as a separate tool.

Procedure:

- All the boards with relevant customer frictions are at the workshop venue.
- In the previous Observe & Learn workshop, the innovation team has selected the most promising five frictions. The participants should therefore be divided into five groups.
- Assign each group ten minutes to generate as many solutions as possible for these customer frictions and to write down their ideas (in a few key words) on a post-it. One idea per post-it. And stick them onto the board.
- Let the groups switch from table to table to brainstorm for a maximum of three minutes to generate additional ideas for other customer frictions.
- Afterwards, the facilitator invites participants of each sub-group to come to the front of the whole group to read their ideas aloud, quickly one after the other, and to post them on the idea wall.
- This continues until all the sub-groups and participants have stuck their post-its on the idea wall and there are no more ideas left.

4.4 Presumptions

This is a creative technique whereby the presumptions implied by the assignment or challenge are made clear, discussed and eliminated. The presumption technique can be applied best at the beginning of the divergence phase in order to reverse the habitual conventions in the product market or within the company.
Duration: 45 minutes

Procedure:

The facilitator asks:

- What are the key concepts of the assignment?
- Allow the participants to write down the key concepts for themselves.
- Allow the participants to mention these key concepts.
- Choose the most important three to five key concepts.
- The facilitator makes a list of the presumptions for each key concept.
- The facilitator asks the participants to eliminate the presumptions.
- The facilitator then asks the participants to invent new ideas without the presumptions and write them on post-its.
- The facilitator continues until there are no more new ideas.
- Continue with the next key concept until the harvest has been exhausted.
- The facilitator invites two participants to come to the front of the group to read their ideas aloud, quickly one after the other, and to post them on the idea wall. This continues until all the participants have stuck their post-its on the idea wall and there are no more ideas left.

4.5 SCAMPER

SCAMPER is an acronym, which consists of the first letters of the seven different approaches which can be used to change a product or service. Bob Eberle developed this technique. It is very useful when brainstorming for new products. It can be compared to the presumptions technique, but is easier to apply for new products.
Duration: 1 hour

Procedure:

> SCAMPER identifies seven main approaches:

- S = Substitute. What can I replace in the composition, the material, the appearance and the size etc. of the product?
- C = Combine. What can I combine with the product to improve it?
- A = Adapt. Can I adapt the product to something else or can I copy something from other sectors?
- M = Magnify/Minimize/Modify? What can I magnify, minimize or modify about the product?
- P = Put to other uses. Can I use the product for something else?
- E = Eliminate. What can I eliminate?
- R = Reverse/Rearrange. Is there anything I can reverse, turn inside out or do in a different order?
- Generate ideas by tackling the questions one by one presented in the seven approaches of SCAMPER.
- The facilitator recites all the questions for each approach.
- The facilitator asks the participants to create new ideas and write them down on a post-it.
- The facilitator invites two participants to come to the front of the group to read their ideas aloud, quickly one after the other, and to post them on the idea wall. This continues until all the participants have stuck their post-its on the idea wall and there are no more ideas left.

4.6 Flower Association

The basic principle of association is that one thought conjures up another thought. A flower association is the first investigation into the context of a specific word in the assignment. The associations are put down on paper around the central word like the petals of a flower. A flower association is usually one of the first creative techniques.

Duration: 30 - 45 minutes

Procedure:
> Determine the core concepts.
- What are the core concepts in the assignment or in the market?
- Allow the participants to write down the core concepts.
- Allow the participants to name the core concepts.
- Choose the most important three to five core concepts.
> Do the flower association.
  Questions:
  - What do you associate this concept with?
  - What type of aspects does the concept have?
  - What does the concept remind you of?
> Write down all the words (like flower petals) around the concept, which is centrally placed.
- The facilitator asks the participants to create new ideas based on the associations and write them down on a post-it.
- The facilitator invites two participants to come to the front of the group to read their ideas aloud, quickly one after the other, and to post them on the idea wall. This continues until all the participants have stuck their post-its onto the idea wall and there are no more ideas left.
- The facilitator continues with the subsequent concepts and flower associations.

4.7 Biomimicry

Biomimicry is derived from bios (life) and mimesis (imitate, copy). Biomimicry is a relatively young science, which studies nature and uses it as a source of inspiration for the challenges with which people are confronted. Janine Benyus, the promoter of Biomimicry, wrote about it in 1997 *Biomimicry: Innovation Inspired by Nature*. Biomimicry is commonly used to solve technical (design) problems.

Duration: 30 minutes

Procedure:
> The facilitator asks:
- If you take the assignment (or the product, or the customer) as the starting point, which animal or object does it resemble in your mind?
> The facilitator writes down the names of these animals or objects.
- The facilitator then chooses one animal or object. Choose one that is familiar to everyone and gives the most inspiration.
> Relate back to new product ideas based on some of the characteristics.
- What are the characteristics of the animal or object?
- Use these characteristics as a source of inspiration for new product ideas and ask the participants to write it on a post-it.
- The facilitator continues until there are no more new ideas.
- Continue with the next characteristic until all have been completed.

4.8 Comic Book Hero

In comic books everything is possible. The heroes are not bothered by the fixed patterns of reality. And this is exactly what we are trying to attain when we brainstorm. We stimulate our own fantasies by 'crawling into the skin' of our favorite childhood comic book heroes.
Duration: 30 minutes

Procedure:
> The facilitator asks:
- What was your favorite comic book hero when you were young?
> Relate back to the innovation assignment via the imaginary hero.

- Put yourself in the place of the comic book hero. Which new product ideas would Asterix or Donald Duck create? Ask the participants to write these ideas on post-its.
- The facilitator continues until there are no more new ideas.

Tip: Should the participants not have any specific comic book hero, then you can ask them about a fairy tale figure or a movie star they liked when they were young.

4.9 Silly Things

You confront the participants with an object, which lies completely outside the context or theme of the brainstorming session, such as a garden gnome, baby rattle or binoculars. The object strikes everyone as so odd that it inspires.
Duration: 30 minutes

Procedure:
> The facilitator passes around a completely random object, which has nothing to do with the product or the market.
> The participants study the object and are then asked to think about the specific characteristics of it.
> Relate back to the assignment based on these characteristics.
- What are the characteristics of this object?
- Use the characteristics as a source of inspiration for new product ideas and ask the participants to write them on post-its.
- The facilitator continues until there are no more new ideas.

4.10 The Insight Game

The Insight Game is a divergence technique whereby new ideas are generated around the most important customer frictions (which were discovered during the focus groups in the Observe and Learn stage) in combination with the strengths of the organization. For this technique you can make a board game that might need to be adapted to fit the circumstances. The participants work in groups of three or four.
Duration: 90 minutes

Procedure:
- Choose the most relevant customer frictions. All the customer friction boards from the Observe and Learn stage are on display in the brainstorming room. Each participant receives four stickers, which have to be placed on those customer frictions he or she thinks are most favorable in light of the assignment. During the FORTH method this takes place in the last Observe & Learn workshop.
- Choose the strengths of the organization.
- Each participant receives green post-its on which they write a maximum of four strengths of the company, which can serve as a competitive advantage in light of the assignment. The facilitator then sticks the post-its onto the wall. Each participant receives four stickers and places them on the strengths considered most favorable in light of the assignment.
- Play the game.
- Each group is given a four-by-four matrix with the client frictions in the rows and the strengths of the company in the columns. Number it one to sixteen. Write the customer frictions and strengths on it.
- Play the board game.
  - The facilitator divides the participants in groups of three or four. Each group receives a board game, a die and a pawn.
  - Player one throws the die and moves the number of squares indicated on the die. The player then lands on a square, which is a combination of an insight and a strength. The players brainstorm together over the combination and jot down their ideas on a post-it.

- Should the brainstorming end, player two throws the die and the game is repeated.
- The combinations, which have already been used, are crossed out and you continue until all sixteen squares have been used.
- At the end of the game the players choose the three squares, which have generated product ideas with the most potential. These are then shared with the group when the facilitator invites participants of each subgroup to come to the front of the whole group to read their ideas aloud, quickly one after the other, and to post them on the idea wall. This continues until all the subgroups and participants have stuck their post-its on the wall and there are no more ideas left.

4.11 Crawl into the skin of

With this brainstorming technique, ideas are generated by crawling into the skin of another person in the target group. When the participants imagine themselves in their new role as 'this other person' new ideas are then created.
Duration: 45 minutes

Procedure:
> Ask the participants, perhaps using the flower association technique, to distinguish the 'types' or 'characters' in the target group.
> For the consumer market:
- the seemingly uninterested adolescent;
- the energetic 70-year-old who is traveling the world;
- the 24/7 X-Box gamer;
- the beer-drinking neighborhood biker (with all due respect).
> For the business-to-business market, for example the energy market:
- the desperate buyer who is taking great risks with rising energy prices;

- the manufacturing manager for whom continuity is the most important aspect;
- the controller who does not want to deviate when it comes to cost price calculations;
- the director who does not want to spend one penny more on energy than necessary.
> Ask either individual participants or the groups of three to four, to crawl into the skin of a real person to the fullest extent possible, including a name, address, daily activity, work, hobby etc. Stimulate them to imitate their chosen 'type'. By using caricatures it eases the imagining process, causes great pleasure and through exaggeration it generates effective perspectives for new ideas.
> Ask individual participants (after they have finished laughing) to create new ideas through this 'new person' and to write them down on a post-it.
> Harvest the post-its.

4.12 What would Apple do?

With this brainstorming technique ideas are generated by crawling into the skin of another company, organization or group like Apple, IKEA, McDonald's or Toyota. When the participants imagine themselves as working for this company, ideas are created in their new role.
Duration: 45 minutes

Procedure:
- Select the organizations. Choose the ones you suspect will add new perspectives to your innovation challenge.
- Ask the groups of three to four, to crawl into the skin of these organizations. Stimulate them to imitate their chosen 'type'. By using caricatures it eases the imagining process, causes great

pleasure and through exaggeration it generates effective per-spectives for new ideas.
- Ask the individual participants (after they have finished laugh-ing) to create new ideas for their innovation assignment from the perspective of being the other organization and to write them down on a post-it. What would Apple do?
- Harvest the post-its.

4.13 Trends Dance

This brainstorming technique brings you far outside the box com-bining various future trends. It gets people moving and dancing to generate high energy and is very well suited for the last idea gen-eration tool.
Duration: 60 minutes

Procedure:
- Select as many future trends as there are participants and write these trends down on a card that the participants can hang around their necks giving them free use of their hands to write ideas on post-its.
- Make a good match distributing the trends among the partici-pants according to their interests and expertise.
- In the first step you ask them individually to come up with as many new ideas as possible based on the trend on their card.
- In the second step you put on loud dancing music. The partici-pants dance. And when the music stops they team up in pairs. Their assignment is to come up with as many ideas as possible based on the trends on both their cards.
- You repeat this several times.
- In the third step you put on loud dancing music. The partici-pants dance. And when the music stops each participant teams up with two others. Their assignment is to come up with as many ideas as possible based on three trends.

- You repeat this several times until the idea flow stagnates.
- The facilitator invites two participants to come to the front of the group to read their ideas aloud, quickly one after the other, and to stick them on the post-it wall. The facilitator asks the rest of the participants to listen well and write down any new ideas on a post-it. This continues until all the participants have stuck their post-its onto the idea wall and there are no more ideas left.

5. IDEA SELECTION TOOLS

5.1 Pinpoint Ideation Directions

The convergence phase starts with pinpointing the directions that our ideas take. On Day One of a brainstorming session you can expect to find 500 - 750 post-its on the idea wall. This technique helps you to link those post-its to specific directions.
Duration: 45 minutes, depending on the number of post-its.

Procedure:
· The facilitator asks the participants to closely examine the post-its wall. The facilitator explains that, for now, the participants need to focus on choosing the two post-its which they believe are the most promising. The remaining ideas will be held onto, as part of the brainstorming session at the end of this stage. Allow five to ten minutes for everyone to carefully study the impressive idea wall. Ask them to choose one post-it which is 'close to home' and a second one which is 'far from home'. This will give you a good mix of feasible solutions and outside-the-box ideas.
· The facilitator asks the participants to read out the selected post-its. Subsequently, the group chooses a title to give to each ideation direction. The facilitator follows the same procedure for each selected post-it. Post-its which are linked to the same direction are placed next to each other on the idea wall. The facilitator continues until the group has the impression that they've exhausted all possible ideation directions. At a new product brainstorming session it is common to come up with 30 to 40 different ideation directions.
· In past brainstorming sessions, we would group all 500+ post-its under different titles of ideation direction. However, this procedure turned out to be very time intensive. These days, we proceed directly to selecting the most promising ideation directions. We have found that doing it this way in practice does not compromise the quality of the final concepts.

5.2 Select ideation directions

This technique often follows the previous phase where 30 to 40 ideation directions are titled and categorized into groups. In this technique you proceed to select the twelve directions with the most potential and developing them further in the next stage using idea mind maps.
Duration: 30 minutes, depending on the number of directions.

Procedure:
· The facilitator hands out stickers and asks the participants to stick them on the ideation direction they believe to have the most potential. In other words, they must choose the ideation direction, which they would like to develop into a new concrete product or service idea. Each participant is not allowed to put more than one sticker on an ideation direction.
· After this step is completed, the facilitator determines, in collaboration with the internal client and the project leader, which directions are the most promising. The principle that works best is: the ones with the most stickers have the most potential. I recommend giving the internal client a 'wild card' so that he or she can also make a choice, which just might give a 'hidden gem' a second chance.
· The selected twelve ideation directions are then developed into idea mind maps.

Tip: The number of stickers depends on the number of directions. Experience has taught that giving each participant seven stickers to distribute over 30 - 40 ideation directions, gives a good representation of the stronger and weaker ideation directions.

5.3 Idea mind mapping

Mind mapping is a well-known brainstorming technique made popular by Tony Buzan, an English psychologist. To make a mind map, place the main theme in the center enclosed in a circle. Key words associated with the central theme are added around it. It's common to use different colors and add drawings. It's a simple technique and the fact that it is very visual makes it easier and quicker for everybody to see the connections between the ideas related to the central theme.
Duration: 45 minutes

Procedure:
· The facilitator explains how mind mapping works and discusses the mind map sheet. On a flip-over page, the ideation direction is written on a post-it and placed in the center. It already has three subdivisions: 'what?', 'for whom?', and 'how?'. There are twelve blank mind map sheets, one for each ideation direction.
· The facilitator gives the participants a marker and asks them to write down or draw everything they associate with the central idea. Judgment, of course, should be deferred until a later stage.
· The participants are given 30 minutes to enrich the twelve idea mind maps with their ideas about their development.
· As soon as everyone has completed this, the facilitator asks the participants to each read out an idea mind map. Doing this exercise gives everybody a good image of the possible developments for each idea.

5.4 With ketchup?

New concepts are presented one by one in a sales pitch or three-minute verbal explanation. The purpose of this technique is to improve the concepts.

Duration: 5 minutes per product idea

Procedure:
· The facilitator asks one of the participants to present the concept to the whole group in three minutes.
· The facilitator asks the rest of the participants if they have any ideas how to strengthen the concept and to write these ideas down on a post-it.
· After the facilitator discusses the additional ideas, they are posted onto the concept board.
· The facilitator continues with the next concept board and the procedure is repeated until all the concepts have been presented.

5.5 Salt and Pepper

The purpose of this technique is to improve a good basic idea, by adding salt and pepper seasoning in the form of fresh ideas.
Duration: 20 minutes for each new concept.

Procedure:
· The facilitator, in consultation with each group, singles out one developed concept that by consensus still needs much improvement. One of the participants is asked to explain the idea.
· The facilitator then asks all the participants to walk up to the original idea wall and choose one idea which can function as 'salt and pepper' for the original concept. In other words: 'Choose the idea which can make this concept better.'
· Each participant then explains his or her 'salt and pepper idea'.
· The group discusses this and chooses which elements to add.
· The procedure is repeated with the next idea, group by group.

Tip: Give the group who has developed the concept board the right to choose which ideas will be added and which ideas will not. In this way the group retains ownership of the idea.

5.6 Pros and cons

With the help of this technique you can improve an idea by quickly summing up its pros and cons and brainstorming new solutions for its negative aspects. This technique is similar to 'salt and pepper', but in this case the positive and negative aspects are discussed explicitly.
Timing: 60 minutes for each new concept.

Procedure:
*   The facilitator in consultation with the group chooses which developed product ideas are eligible for further development. The finding of the qualitative research in the Test Ideas stage will provide the answer immediately.
*   The facilitator divides the participants into groups of two or three and in consultation with the project leader then divides the product concepts among the groups. In this way, the groups can simultaneously improve four to eight concepts. The improvements are immediately adapted to the description of the original concept.
*   The participants present the improved concepts to each other. More additions from the group might be added.
*   The procedure is repeated until all eligible concepts have been discussed.

5.7 Multi-criteria selection

The purpose of this technique is to determine the final rank order of the completed new concepts. Which one scores best?
Duration: 60 minutes

Procedure:
*   The facilitator already has evaluation charts prepared. All

boards with the concepts and evaluation charts are displayed on the tables along the wall. The facilitator shows the evaluation chart and discusses the evaluation procedure. This is an important phase, so make sure to allow enough time. It is also good to emphasize to the participants that a lot of thought has gone into the evaluation procedure and that the criteria have been selected in close consultation with the project leader and internal client and are based on the innovation assignment.
*   The facilitator explains that for each developed product idea there are five evaluation criteria. For each criterion the participants have the possibility to give the idea 0 to 5 points (stickers): 0 = low and 5 = high. The categories for each criterion are explained with the help of the evaluation board.
*   The facilitator hands out the sticker sheets with the task to evaluate each product idea according to the five criteria.
*   After the participants have completed their evaluations of all the concept boards, the facilitator signals that it's time to tally the stickers for each board. The facilitator is the first to know the rank order of the most attractive developed product ideas. The results will be kept secret until the facilitator presents them to the group during the grand finale.

5.8 My Valentine

This is a nice technique to add some 'passion' to the final evaluation. With a red, heart-shaped 'I love you' sticker the participants can now give their favorite idea an extra boost with this final evaluation.

Procedure:
*   The facilitator hands out only one 'I love you' sticker to each participant with the request to openly declare which developed product or service idea has stolen his or her heart.

- The participants then stick their heart and evaluation stickers onto the selection boards of their choice.
- At the presentation of the final rank order the facilitator pays attention to how many stickers the concepts received in the previous technique compared to how many hearts the concepts received in this technique.

Tip: In most cases, the hearts go to the concepts which end high in the rank order. If that is not the case, then this striking difference should be pointed out to the group to see if they can find an explanation for this. How is it possible that the concept boards, which received the most hearts, scored so low in the rank order? The participants are allowed to alter the rank order on the basis of a contextual discussion; and should certainly do so if it is justified.

6. BRAINSTORMING GAMES

Brainstorming brings to mind something playful and fun to do. It is therefore not surprising that many games have been created to either brainstorm in a group or individually. The games are usually very simple and often take over the role of the facilitator. Below, you will find four popular games, which can help you to brainstorm on your own or in a group.

Brainstorming games to brainstorm on your own:
- Free the Genie Cards (www.ideachampions.com/free_the_genie.shtml). Free the Genie is a set of 55 creative thinking cards for openminded people.
- The KnowBrainer (www.innovationsecrets.com). A useful fan-deck tool with 180 cards which include questions, quotes, words and images to provide you with inspiration for new ideas.
- Thinkpak (www.creativethinking.net). A set of brainstorming cards by Michael Michalko to stimulate creativity and get new ideas.
- Innovative Whack Pack (www.creativewhack.com). A set of cards made by Roger von Oech with 60 creative ways and inspired by the old Greek philosopher Heraclitus.

Brainstorming games for groups:
- IDEO method cards (http://www.ideo.com/work/item/method-cards). A set of 51 cards by the world famous designing agency IDEO, which contain various ways in which the designer teams can understand the target group better.
- Metaforio (http://www.metaforio.com/english/). An instrument for visual and creative development based on the technique of visual thought. The game consists of a set of 53 inspiring training cards based on the garden metaphor.

7. BRAINSTORM SOFTWARE

Brainstorm software is widely available. There are two main areas of focus: software for mind mapping and software to support the whole process of brainstorming. Below are some examples of both types.

- CREAX Innovation Suite (www.creaxinnovationsuite.com). An extensive and user-friendly package regarding systematic innovation, based on TRIZ from Creax. It offers a step-by-step approach to the whole process of innovation.
- Flashbrainer (www.solutionpeople.com/flashbrainer). A brainstorming program which consists of four steps (Investigate, Create, Evaluate and Activate) and leads you through the innovation process.
- Mindmanager (www.mindjet.com). A well-known and extensive mind map package. It has various editions and all sorts of 'add-ons'.
- Visual Mind (www.visual-mind.com). A software program for mind mapping. An 'add-in' has been made, (The Realizer), which is a practical tool to help you to generate and evaluate ideas.

8. ONLINE BRAINSTORMING

There are many ideation generating tools available on the Internet. They are free of charge and are usually practical and simple instruments to generate new ideas, such as the 'Ideagenerator' described below. Websites where you can mind map online without any software, such as 'Mindmeister', are also popular. Other sites allow you to generate and evaluate ideas immediately online within a group, such as 'Brainreactions' and 'Brainstormnet'.

- Mindmeister (www.mindmeister.com). A mind mapping tool enabling you to create mind maps online and in a group.
- Ideagenerator (www.tdbspecialprojects.com). When you click on the free online idea generator you receive surprising word combinations which can create new ideas within the group.
- Brainreactions (www.brainreactions.net). Online brainstorming rooms, where you can jointly generate and evaluate around a challenge of your choice.

9. TRIZ

TRIZ is a Russian acronym for Teoriya Resheniya Izobreatatel-skikh Zadatch, which means Theory of Inventive Problem Solving. The creator of TRIZ is the Russian engineer Genrich Altshuller. He began the development of his theory in 1946 while working at the patent office of the former Soviet navy. It was there that his fascination began to grow as to how an invention is created. Are inventions unique and brilliant occurrences? Are they coincidental treasures? Or, are there underlying systematic patterns? Altshuller did not believe in the trial-and-error method for which Thomas Edison is known (innovation is 1% inspiration and 99% perspiration)

and began developing a more effective and systematic approach. He became convinced that the basis of inventions lies in systematic patterns. To prove this, he analyzed hundreds of thousands of patents regarding mutuality and repeated patterns. Subsequently, TRIZ scientists have collectively analyzed more than a million patents.

TRIZ is a powerful yet complex methodology that is not easy to comprehend without any technical understanding. The table below gives a description of the 40 TRIZ principles, with a brief explanation and an example of its application in practice.

40 TRIZ PRINCIPLES AS A SOURCE OF INSPIRATION FOR NEW IDEAS

Nr.	Principle	Description	Example
1.	Segmentation, fragmentation or division.	Divide the product into independent parts in order to isolate or integrate useful or harmful characteristics.	A store within a store concept.
2.	Taking out, omission, separation or isolation.	Separate one or more of the interfering or harmful parts or properties and/or use the only necessary property.	Caffeine free coffee.
3.	Local quality.	Change the structure from uniform to non-uniform (locally) of one of the products to get the desired function.	Easy opening of a juice carton.
4.	Asymmetry, symmetry change.	Change the shape of an object from symmetrical to asymmetrical.	A special vase for tulips.
5.	Merging, combining, consolidating, or integrating.	Bring functions, characteristics or parts of a product together in time and space so that a new, desired or unique result is produced.	Mobile telephone with navigation system.
6.	Universality, multi-functionality.	Make a product more uniform, universal, extensive and multi-functional.	A combination screwdriver and drill.
7.	Nested doll.	Products which fit against, next to or in each other.	Stackable lawn chairs.
8.	Anti-weight.	Compensate for a negative aspect of the product with an opposite power from the environment (and so create a uniform division).	Hovercraft.

Nr.	Principle	Description	Example
9.	Preliminary anti-action.	Analyze in advance what can go wrong and then take actions to eliminate, decrease or prevent it.	Sunscreen.
10.	Preliminary action.	Perform an action before another action or event. Do something in advance.	Local anesthetic.
11.	Beforehand cushioning.	Realize that nothing is perfectly trustworthy so compensate in advance.	Paint protectant car wax.
12.	Equipotentiality.	Make sure that there is no tension in or around a system or make everything all equal.	Anti-aging cream.
13.	The other way around.	Apply an opposite or reverse action. Turn it upside down or inside out.	Heinz top-down squeeze bottles.
14.	Curved or spherical shape.	Replace linear aspects (e.g., shape, movement, power) with a curved or spherical shape.	Black & Decker Mouse Sander.
15.	Dynamics.	Make a product, condition or aspect short lived, temporary, moveable, adaptable, flexible or changeable.	Early booking discounts.
16.	A bit more or less, partial or excessive actions.	Use 'a bit more' of one action or substance than necessary and deal with the results. Use a 'little less' of an action or substance than necessary and deal with the results.	Extra thick soup.
17.	Another dimension.	Change the orientation of a linear (straight) product from vertical to horizontal, from horizontal to diagonal, from horizontal to vertical, etc. Work in another dimension or in several layers.	Multi-layered cookies.
18.	Mechanical vibration.	Use shaking, vibrations or oscillations to get a positive effect of a desired function.	Power Plate.
19.	Periodic actions.	Replace continuous actions with periodic or pulsating actions. Change the way in which an action is performed.	Philips Sonic electric toothbrush.
20.	Continuity of useful action.	Create a continuous stream (circulation) and/or remove all useless, interim and unproductive movements to increase the efficiency.	Internet e-tickets.
21.	Hasten, skipping, running ahead.	If something goes wrong at a specific tempo, then do it faster.	Broadband Internet.
22.	Blessing in disguise.	Find ways in which disadvantages can be used to add value. Turn a disadvantage into an advantage.	Slow Food restaurant.

Nr.	Principle	Description	Example
23.	Feedback.	Feed the output of one system back into the system as an input to improve the control of the output.	Telephone number for complaints printed on packaging of products.
24.	Intermediary.	Mediate a temporary connection between incompatible parties, functions, events or conditions. Use a temporary carrier, barrier or a temporary process which can be removed easily again.	Microwave meal packaging.
25.	Self-service.	Allow an object or system to carry out certain functions on its own or to organize it independently.	Online investment.
26.	Copying.	Use a copy, replica or model instead of using something too valuable, vulnerable or unavailable.	Crash simulators for cars via computer models.
27.	Cheap short-living products.	Use cheaper, more simple or disposable objects to decrease the cost, and to increase the user friendliness, etc.	Disposable plates and utensils.
28.	Mechanics substitution.	Replace mechanical interactions with physical fields or with other forms, actions or conditions. This principle is about the changing or replacing of the operational principle of a system.	Motorized bicycle.
29.	Pneumatics and hydraulics.	Replace the components or functions of one system with pneumatic (air) or hydraulic (water) components or functions.	Bicycle Springer Fork.
30.	Flexible shells and thin films.	Replace traditional constructions with constructions of thin films or flexible/pliable membranes.	Hansaplast liquid spray bandage.
31.	Porous materials.	Change the characteristics or functions of an object, system or material (solid, liquid or gas) by making it more porous. Create cavities and add a useful substance or function.	Porous bandage with iodine which allows air to pass through.
32.	Color changes.	Change the color or other optical aspects of an object or system to increase the value of the system or to discover problems.	Tefal Thermo-Spot.
33.	Homogeneity, uniformity.	When two or more objects or substances influence each other, then it is better to consist of the same material, energy or information.	School uniforms.
34.	Discarding and recovering.	Throwing away of parts of a system and recycling is basically the same. Throwing away removes something from the system. Recycling brings something back to the system in order to use it again.	Recycling of packaging.

Nr.	Principle	Description	Example
35.	Parameter changes.	Change the characteristics of a system to gain a useful advantage.	Sprinkler hose pipe.
36.	Phase transition.	Use the phase transition (e.g., from a solid to a liquid or from a liquid to a gas) of one material or situation to implement an effective change or to create a change in the system.	Tea kettle whistle.
37.	Thermal expansion.	Change heat energy into mechanical energy or action.	Bimetallic strip thermometer.
38.	Strong oxidants.	Strengthen oxidative processes to improve an action or function.	Extra oxygen in a cutting torch.
39.	Inert atmosphere.	Create a neutral (inertia) atmosphere or environment to support a desired function.	Vacuum electric oven.
40.	Composite materials.	Change a homogenous structure of a material to a compound structure.	Insulating material.

I would like to express my gratitude to Karel Bolckmans, who helped generate numerous examples.

Sources:
D. Mann, S. Dewulf, B. Zlotin, A. Zusman. (2003). *Matrix 2003: Updating the TRIZ Contradiction Matrix*.
Ieper (Belgium): Creax Press. p. 140 (principles and sub-principles).
G. Altshuller. (2005). *40 Principles: TRIZ Keys to Technical Innovation. Extended Edition*.
Worcester, MA: Technical Innovation Center Inc. p. 143 (descriptions).

10. SIT

SIT stands for Systematic Inventive Thinking. This technique comes from Israel and is closely related to the TRIZ method described above. It is a simple version and can be easily applied. Neither technique is a brainstorming method in the traditional sense; as neither one strays from the existing product situation to invent new, breakthrough product ideas. The SIT and TRIZ methods approach inventions from the opposite perspective and both stay as close as possible to the original product. Many versions of SIT have been developed throughout the years. Depending on the version, SIT works on the basis of five to seven creativity templates. Scientific research has shown that the SIT creativity templates form the basis of roughly 70% of all innovations.

SIT focuses on the existing building blocks of an existing product and its environment. The application of the creativity templates leads to a reorganization of the product's building blocks. SIT first focuses on the change within the product itself and then studies if there has been a positive or negative effect.

SIT works according to seven creativity templates.

1. Displacement: an essential part of the product is removed and the task is not taken over by another part. For example, dehydrate a can of soup and you will have Cup-a-Soup.
2. Replacement: an essential part of the product is removed and the task is taken over by another part. For example, omit the keyboard from a computer and have the screen take over this task and you will have a touch screen.
3. Multiplication: copy an existing part of the product and change something about it. For example, copy the holes which dispense the content from the package of a product and make adjustments to increase the number of garnishing holes.
4. Breaking symmetry: to break through an existing symmetry to solve a problem. For example, to save space in the car, you make a smaller spare tire to drive a limited distance.
5. Attribute dependency: create a new dependability between two parts or remove an existing dependability. For example, make the color of the bottom of the pan dependable on the temperature of the pan and you have the Tefal Thermo-Spot pan (with red spot).
6. Division: divide the product or parts into something else. For example, have customers divided into two groups: store card holders and non card holders and organize special late night shopping evenings for the first group.
7. Unification/Component control: find a new connection between a part of a product and the environment so that the product gets a new extra task which was formerly the task of another product. For example, Becel (Benecol) pro-activ which lowers cholesterol.

The seven creativity templates implicitly put the presumptions of the product combination, its product and its customer groups at the forefront. The SIT creativity templates also have an added value as a trigger for new ideas in the divergence phase of brainstorming for new products. It is best to apply the SIT creativity templates at the beginning of the divergence phase.

Source:
Van Logtestijn, Annina, Youri Mandour. (March 2004). *"Zeven stappen naar succesvollere innovaties." Tijdschrift voor Marketing.*

11. 6 THINKING HATS

The six thinking hats is a technique developed by Edward de Bono. The added value of this technique during the creation of new products or services is that an idea can be improved upon by putting on different thinking hats. Using this technique, possible improvement suggestions can be devised.

Duration: Approximately 3 to 4 hours for each concrete new product in development.

Procedure:

> The facilitator explains the principles of the six thinking hats, which are actually quite simple. The different angles of approach produce a more complete image combined than any individual angle would on its own. The basics of the different thinking hats are as follows:

· The white thinking hat: pristine white thoughts in the form of facts, figures and information.

· The red thinking hat: a red haze blurring one's vision in the form of emotions and sentimental evaluation as well as suspicions and intuition.

· The yellow thinking hat: sunshine, clarity and optimism, positive evaluation, constructive contribution, searching for chances (opportunistic).

· The green thinking hat: fertility, creativity, seeds which germinate and grow, movement, provocation. Alternative and new ideas are welcome.

· The black thinking hat: the devil's advocate, negative evaluation, why something will not function.

· The blue thinking hat (the hat of the facilitator): distant and controlled, the conductor of the thought process, thinking about the thinking.

> The facilitator finds four spots in the available working space and puts down a white, red, black and yellow hat and a flip-over

sheet. The blue hat is for the facilitator and the green hat will be used collectively at the end.

> The participants are divided into four groups (minimum of two people). Each group starts with a thinking hat of a specific color and everyone must also wear the hat! The facilitator asks the participants to write down their impressions of the new product idea from their specific angle of approach. After ten minutes the participants must change stations. The hat and the flip-over sheet are left behind for the next group to use. This continues until each group has completed each angle of approach.

> After 40 minutes, the facilitator hangs the white, red, yellow and black sheets on the wall and discusses the results with the participants. The sheet for the black hat must be done at the end.

> Subsequently, the facilitator asks the participants to put on the green thinking hat collectively and start finding solutions for each negative aspect or disadvantage of the product idea. These solutions are then written on green post-its and the facilitator harvests the post-its. The best solution for the weakness is chosen.

> The group then continues with the product's next weakness. New aspects and changes which can lead to substantial improvements now strengthen the original product or service ideas.

Marvelous Innovation Books

Clayton M. Christensen (1997). *The Innovator's Dilemma*. Boston, MA: Harvard Business School Press.

David E. Hussey (1997). *The Innovation Challenge*. New York, NY: John Wiley & Sons.

Harvard Business Review (1997). *On Innovation*. Boston, MA: Harvard Business School Press.

Ernest Gundling (2000). *The 3M Way to Innovation, Balancing People and Profit*. Tokyo: Kodansha International.

Robert Jones (2001). *The Big Idea*. London: HarperCollins Publishers.

Shira White (2002). *New Ideas about New Ideas*. New York, NY: Perseus Publishing.

Elaine Dundon (2002). *The Seeds of Innovation*. New York, NY: American Management Association.

Jonathan Cagan & Craig M. Vogel (2002). *Creating Breakthrough Products – Innovation from Product Planning to Program Approval*. Upper Saddle River, NJ: FT Press.

Clayton M. Christensen & Michael E. Raynor (2003). *The Innovator's Solution: Creating and Sustaining Successful Growth*. Boston, MA, Harvard Business School Publishing Corporation.

W. Chan Kim & Renee Mauborgne (2005). *Blue Ocean Strategy*. Boston, MA, Harvard Business School Publishing Corporation.

Anthony Ulwick (2005). *What Customers Want*. New York, NY McGraw-Hill.

Chris Barez-Brown (2006). *How to Have Kick-Ass Ideas*. London: HarperCollins Publishers.

David Nichols (2007). *Return On Ideas – A Practical Guide to Make Innovation Pay*. New York, NY: John Wiley & Sons.

Igor Byttebier, Ramon Vullings (2007). *Creativity Today*. Amsterdam: BIS Publishers.

Michael Dahlen (2008). *Creativity Unlimited*. West Sussex: John Wiley & Sons.

Tim Hurson (2008). *Think Better*. New York, NY: Mc Graw Hill.

Henry Chesbrough, Wim Vanhaverbeke, Joel West (2008). *Open Innovation*. Oxford: Oxford University Press.

Denis J. Hauptly (2008). *Something Really New*. New York, NY: American Management Association.

Bettina von Stamm, Anna Trifilova (2009). *The Future of Innovation*. Surrey: Gower Publishing Company.

Marc Stickdorn & Jakob Schneider (2010). *This is Service Design Thinking*. Amsterdam: BIS Publishers.

Alexander Osterwalder, Yves Pigneur (2010). *Business Model Generation*. Hoboken, NJ: John Wiley & Sons.

Robert Cooper (2011). *Winning at New Products*. New York, NY: Basic Books.

Henry Chesbrough (2011). *Open Services Innovation*. San Francisco, CA: Jossey-Bass.

Inspiring Exploration Books

Roald Amundsen (1999). *Roald Amundsen's Belgica Diary*. Alburgh, UK: Archival Facsimiles.

Ernest Shackleton (1999). *South: The Endurance Expedition*. New York, NY: Penguin Putnam.

Sir Edmund Hillary (2000). *View from the Summit*. New York, NY: Simon & Schuster.

Roald Amundsen (2001). *The South Pole*. New York, NY: Cooper Square Press.

George Plimpton (2005). *As Told at the Explorers Club: More Than Fifty Gripping Tales of Adventure*. Guilford, UK: Lyons Press.

James R. Hanssen (2005). *First Man, the Life of Neil A. Armstrong*. New York, NY: Simon & Schuster.

Robin Hanbury-Tenison (2010). *The Great Explorers*. London, UK: Thames & Hudson ltd.

Royal Geographical Society, Alasdair Macleod (2010). *Explorers* . London, UK: Dorling Kindersley ltd.

Stewart Ross (2011). *Into the Unknown*. Somerville, UK: Candlewick Press.

Martin Howard (2011). *Christopher Columbus*. London, UK: A & C Black Publishers.

David Boyle (2011). *Voyages of Discovery*. London, UK: Thames & Hudson Ltd.

I like to thank all photographers on Flickr (www.flickr.com) who granted permission to copy, distribute, transmit and adapt their work under Creative Commons.

Page 7	This photo is used under Creative Commons from Rennett Stowe.
Page 8	This photo is used under Creative Commons from Wolfgang Photo.
Page 14	This is a detail of an image by W.H. Overend, 1876.
Page 16	This photo is used under Creative Commons from Beshef.
Page 17	This photo is used under Creative Commons from Beshef.
Page 18	Artist: L. Prang & Co., 1893, Boston. This image is in the public domain because of its age.
Page 21	The designer and/or photographer of the map are unknown.
Page 23	Map made by Jodocus Hondius. Photo credits: The collections of the Royal Geographical Society.
Page 26	Photo credits: National Library of Norway.
Page 27	Photo credits: National Library of Norway.
Page 28	Photo credits: National Library of Norway.
Page 29	Photo credits: National Library of Norway.
Page 31	This photo is used under Creative Commons from ilkerender.
Page 32	This photo is used under Creative Commons from Göran Höglund.
Page 34	This photo is used under Creative Commons from Charles Atkeison.
Page 35	This photo is used under Creative Commons from Phaedrus.
Page 36	Photo credits: NASA.
Page 37	Photo credits: NASA.
Page 38	Photo credits: The collections of the Royal Geographical Society.
Page 39	Photo credits: The collections of the Royal Geographical Society.
Page 45	Photo credits: The collections of the Royal Geographical Society.
Page 46	This photo is used under Creative Commons from Steve Jurvetson.
Page 48	This photo is used under Creative Commons from Nosha.
Page 50	This photo is used under Creative Commons from Michael Gil.
Page 59	This photo is used under Creative Commons from Reed Kennedy.
Page 65	This photo is used under Creative Commons from Nelson Minar.
Page 80	Photo credits: The US Army.
Page 88	This photo is used under Creative Commons from fdecomite.
Page 91	This photo is used under Creative Commons from Johan Larsson.
Page 93	This photo is used under Creative Commons from Alexandre van de Sande.
Page 97	Van Schagen's map of the world, 1689. This image is in the public domain because of its age.
Page 100	This photo is used under Creative Commons from ND Strupler.
Page 102	This photo is used under Creative Commons from Rachel D.
Page 108	This photo is used under Creative Commons from Wolfgang Staudt.
Page 110	This photo is used under Creative Commons from Oliver.
Page 117	This photo is used under Creative Commons from Kovalcheck.
Page 118	This photo is used under Creative Commons from Felipe Gabaldon.
Page 122	This photo is used under Creative Commons from Steven Jones.
Page 126	This photo is used under Creative Commons from Nimish Gogri.
Page 131	This photo is used under Creative Commons from JD Hancock.
Page 134	This photo is used under Creative Commons from Stig Nygaard.
Page 144	This photo is used under Creative Commons from Camilla Nilsson.
Page 150	This photo is used under Creative Commons from Alain Levine.
Page 156	This photo is used under Creative Commons from The Impulsive Buy.
Page 158	This photo is used under Creative Commons from Tripp.
Page 163	This photo is used under Creative Commons from Kyle May.
Page 164	Photo credits: NASA.
Page 171	This photo is used under Creative Commons from Noel Reynolds.
Page 172	Checklist Gemini XII. This photo is used under Creative Commons from Erik Charlton.
Page 176	This photo is used under Creative Commons from Donnie Ray Jones.
Page 180	This photo is used under Creative Commons from Christoph Mendt.
Page 185	This photo is used under Creative Commons from Mr. Wabu.
Page 188	This photo is used under Creative Commons from Boegh.
Page 193	Mood board. This photo is used under Creative Commons from Julie Gibbons.
Page 198	This photo is used under Creative Commons from Rich Moffit.
Page 201	Photo credits: MyShelter Foundation.
Page 202	This photo is used under Creative Commons from Maureen.
Page 205	This photo is used under Creative Commons from Cristian Bortes.
Page 207	This photo is used under Creative Commons from Philip Leara.
Page 210	This photo is used under Creative Commons from Dean Souglass.
Page 213	This photo is used under Creative Commons from Steve Jurvetson.
Page 216	This photo is used under Creative Commons from Daniel Richter.